The Western Alliance

*A Publication of the Social Science Division of the
Mershon Center for Education in National Security*

Edited by Edgar S. Furniss, Jr.

The Western Alliance   *Its Status and Prospects*

OHIO STATE UNIVERSITY PRESS

Foreword

The following is excerpted from the remarks of Frederic Heimberger in introducing one of the speakers in this series on the Western Alliance. Dr. Heimberger is professor emeritus of political science and former vice-president for instruction and research at the Ohio State University.

COLONEL RALPH D. MERSHON, a native of Zanesville, Ohio, enrolled in this university in 1886 as a member of the fourteenth freshman class to be admitted. He graduated in 1890 with a degree in mechanical engineering and went on to become a very successful consulting engineer, chiefly concerned with transmitting electric power over longer distances than had ever before been practical. But with all of his heavy professional commitments, Colonel Mershon found time for two other abiding interests. One was his university, and largely through his effort the Alumni Association was established as a powerful force in its development. The other strong interest was in his country and all of its broader meanings in terms of freedom, opportunity, and the importance of the individual.

His devotion to this land and what it stands for was coupled with a stern sense of duty, of ready acceptance of the responsibilities that rightfully fall upon every citizen—

civilian as well as soldier—who enjoys and cherishes the blessings of a free nation. In death, Colonel Mershon left to this university the great bulk of his personal fortune. His will indicated Colonel Mershon's strong belief in the future of this country by requesting that the principal of the trust remain invested in common stocks. He also desired that any program funded by his bequest be in addition to the regular pursuits of a university, for he expressly provided that the income was not to relieve the state government of its obligation to provide funds for "routine" university expenditures. Finally, he suggested the development of a specific program by stating that at least one-half of the income was to be used for endeavors that, in the sole judgment of the University, would advance civilian-military education in the United States and its territories.

Although Colonel Mershon wisely left the determination of specific projects and methods to the good judgment of those who came after him, his central purposes can be discovered quite easily through a study of his writings and, particularly, the patterns of his life. Stated very briefly, his first goal was the security of this nation and all that it stands for in a troubled world. His second was the acceptance of full responsibility by those whose pursuits might be primarily civilian in nature but who must not—and indeed cannot—neglect the stern duties of defense, whatever changing forms they may take with changing times. His own life as an innovator who was ready at all times to push beyond the known and currently accepted ways of doing things has set a clear example for those seeking new and possibly even daring approaches to the equally new situations and problems that face all men in their quest for the security of what they cherish most.

His handsome bequest carries with it a continuing obligation and a matchless opportunity. The obligation is to keep faith with the donor in every year forward. The opportunity is to seek freely and fearlessly for those new solutions that may be neglected by others but which, eventually, may best serve his original purposes. It is even more than an opportunity. It is a challenge to break through the constrictions of the past as he knew it—to find new answers for the new day that must always lie ahead.

This has been the spirit of those who have guided the affairs of the Mershon program. Although clearly recognizing the current need for national security through national force, they have had no illusions about the steadily decreasing ability of any nation to defend itself alone in this day and age. Instead, they have properly regarded the force of arms as essentially a protective shield and have sought diligently to strengthen the arsenal of all free men in those other and more enduring weapons of knowledge, reason, association, and enforceable law. It is within this broad framework of ideas that the Mershon Center for Education in National Security has been developed and now operates on many fronts and in many ways—conferences, seminars, fellowships, research, publications, and distinguished lecturers.

Acknowledgments

THE CHAPTERS IN THIS VOLUME represent revised versions of manuscripts originally read as addresses to weekly colloquia held during the winter of 1965 at the Ohio State University. The series on the Western Alliance constituted one of the major activities of the academic year 1964-65 of the Social Science Program of the Mershon Center for Education in National Security. In addition to delivering the addresses and presiding over their adaptation for publication, the authors participated in private discussions of Alliance affairs with members of the Mershon Center. The editor happily records his gratitude to the eight distinguished men of affairs whose thoughts are presented in these pages. He adds his heartfelt thanks to General Lauris Norstad for his active interest in and significant contributions to this enterprise from its very inception. Finally, he wishes to acknowledge his debt in this, as in other concerns of the Social Science Program, to Professor Robert J. Nordstrom, chairman of the Mershon Committee.

E. S. F.

Contents

The Western Alliance

Dirk Stikker

The Role of the Secretary General of NATO

I THINK THAT the best way to deal with my subject is first to describe very briefly the vast variety of subjects with which NATO must occupy itself; then to describe (again briefly) the terms of reference of the Secretary General; and, finally, to give some examples of the practical problems for which the Secretary General, together with the Council, individual members, and military authorities, has to find solutions. As examples of this exhausting task, I have chosen Cyprus, the diminishing will of France under De Gaulle to co-operate in NATO, and the great problem of strategy and nuclear weapons.

I

NATO is a vast organization; nothing comparable to it ever existed in time of peace. Every day, the men and women of NATO, the staffs of the permanent delegations of the member countries, and the members of the International Staff, prepare, often in committee meetings, the work of the Permanent Council. All these people must have a very high degree of skill, of loyalty to their own countries and to NATO, and, in the case of the International Secretariat, complete objectivity.

The delegations must continuously be fully aware of the political trends and thinking in their countries, and they must be able to speak at any moment on their government's policy, sometimes, in case of urgency, without preparation. This means that every day, in the various capitals and in Paris, several thousands of people are engaged in preparing the work of the Council.

NATO wants peace, and therefore NATO must always be ready to do its job for the preservation of the peace. When member countries still consider it necessary, as they do at the present moment, to keep a total of about six million men under arms and to maintain defense budgets of more than $70 billion, it is clear that the political situation is still such that the NATO Council must be able to meet and act at any moment.

In normal circumstances, the Council meets at least once a week, (and very often three or four times a week) under deliberately flexible rules of procedure, to consult or to bind governments in decisions. There are usually about one hundred fifty people, including aides and experts, in the room, speaking English or French. The agenda may list any of these topics at any time.

1. Foreign policy in the widest sense, without any geographical limitation

2. Information

3. Disarmament

4. Armament, standardization, and joint production

5. Scientific developments

6. Civil defense

7. Strategy

8. Military requirements

9. Military exercises

10. Construction of pipelines (8,000 miles in Europe alone), airfields (several hundred), radar systems and means of communication (and—what may be rather surprising—we never had a scandal)

11. Intelligence

12. Burden-sharing

13. Budget control

14. Trade relations and long-term and short-term credit policy

15. Staff and personnel policy

This is only a rough outline of the different fields of activity; discussions in the Council may go in detail into any of these subjects.

The Secretary General presides at all meetings of the Council, be it on the level of permanent representatives, heads of government, or ministers of foreign affairs, defense, or finance. It is the task of the Secretary General to summarize the discussions and formulate conclusions and, when possible, decisions.

II

What are the rights and duties given to the Secretary General that enable him to fulfill this task?

There does not exist a comprehensive document to describe his task. The position was created in 1952, and later, in 1956, its responsibilities were greatly enlarged. But the decision to increase the scope of his function gives only part of the story, because over the years the Secretary General's task has grown with the steady expansion of the Council's activities.

The Council is the highest authority in NATO; the responsibilities of the Secretary General spring mainly from his serving as chairman of the Council and all ministerial sessions. He conducts the discussions, maintains order, prepares the agendas, and, being head of the International Secretariat, represents the organization in all agencies acting under authorization of the Council.

If I limit myself to the Secretary General's duties in time of peace, the following summing-up of his duties and rights seems valid.

In the Military Field

The Council gives political directives to military authorities and asks these authorities for advice.

The preparation, even to the extent of initiative, and the execution of any Council decision in this field rest with the Secretary General.

The Secretary General has access to all military agencies and commanders, but—a strange fact—he has no personal military adviser.

It is the Secretary's duty, if necessary through direct contacts with governments, to ascertain actual compliance with military requirements.

He must present military appraisal to the Ministerial Meeting once a year.

He must maintain contacts with certain other political-military organizations, like the Western European Union, CENTO, and SEATO, and also with the Council of Europe.

In the Political and Economic Fields

The Secretary General sees to it that all items coming up for discussion in the Council are prepared in explanatory and objective documents.

The Secretary General has (and this is perhaps his most important function) the right of initiative, which gives to his position a certain amount of supranational character.

All governments have accepted the obligation to keep the Secretary General informed regarding their policies and therefore, several governments allow him to read regularly their political telegrams and reports.

He has the right to correspond with governments, and he regularly visits all capitals.

Although without any power to commit the Alliance or any specific country, he is the official spokesman for NATO, and he meets constantly with the press, appears on television and radio, writes articles, speaks to parliamentarians of NATO and WEU, and gives lectures in all fifteen countries.

It is his task to help countries in need of economic and defense aid, such as Greece and Turkey.

Once a year he must present to ministers an analysis and appraisal of existing political and economic problems and make recommendations to them on how these problems could be solved.

He has the right and the duty to bring to the attention of the Council all matters which in his opinion may threaten the solidarity and effectiveness of the Alliance.

He can offer his good offices to member governments in dispute, initiating—if his offer is accepted—procedures of inquiry, mediation, conciliation, or arbitration.

The International Secretariat

The Secretary General is the head of the International Secretariat of about one thousand; he appoints and dismisses staff and organizes the work. In the matter of his staff policy, he is dependent on the Council only for the funds which governments make available to him.

Security

The Secretary General is responsible for security throughout the organization and is in constant contact with security agencies of member countries.

Finance

He is responsible for financial and budgetary control of the organization.

This was, roughly speaking, in the last years (in a time of peace), my job; you will readily understand that there was always something to do. Fourteen hours a day, seven days a week, was normal routine. I had always to be near a telephone; I never had a real holiday; and I had to take action even when I was ill.

It was a fascinating job, especially since I was surrounded by an excellent and most loyal staff, always ready to strengthen and increase our efforts to maintain the peace, whatever difficulties might arise. But you will understand that at one of my last meetings with the military authorities I was justified in using the expression, "Life is one damn thing after the other!"

I left this demanding, but deeply rewarding, work for reasons of health. I am happy (and I envy him for it) that my successor has such good health.

You will understand that in functions of this kind what is generally accepted as a desirable minimum of private life is nonexistent: social contacts—which many politicians and ambassadors crave—and even family life are all subordinated to the unending demands of the job.

III

Let me now turn to a few concrete examples of how these rights and duties of the Secretary General have been performed in practice in dealing with problems facing the Council, the member countries, and military authorities.

Cyprus

In 1951, two countries were reluctant to agree to the admission of Greece and Turkey to NATO: these were Denmark and the Netherlands, where I was then the Foreign Minister. In that period, I had some doubts whether these countries of the near Middle East could really be considered Atlantic. Did they belong to a North Atlantic grouping? If Great Britain, France, and the United States considered it so important to have them as their allies, would it not be better to make a separate pact, as was later the case with CENTO and SEATO. Moreover, for ages there had been conflict in that part of the world over the control of the Aegean Sea, and between Islam and the Orthodox church.

Finally, when the three leading powers of NATO insisted on their admission, I, as minister of one of the smaller countries, did not want to oppose; and when I gave way, Denmark also agreed.

The Cyprus issue was certainly not in my mind at that time and it was only as a member of the Council that I had reason to go deeper into the history of this unhappy island.

At the division of the Roman Empire, Cyprus went to the Byzantine Empire; later it was successively under the control of Genoa, Venice, and Egypt. In the fourteenth and fifteenth centuries Cyprus was a kingdom, where once the king was at the same time archbishop. From 1573 to 1878, it belonged to the Ottoman Empire. In 1878, when Turkey was threatened by Russia, England intervened, (the world was then living under the Pax Britannica) and, in exchange for its guarantees against Russian invasion, obtained from Turkey the right to occupy Cyprus. During World War I, Great Britain annexed Cyprus and offered it to Greece if Greece would support Serbia against Bulgaria, which Greece refused to do. Cyprus then became a British Crown colony and was recognized as such in the Treaty of Lausanne of 1924.

It was in 1931 that, under the leadership of the Orthodox church, agitation for "enosis," union with Greece, started. During World War II, the island was not occupied by the Germans, and after the war it remained a British Crown colony, but it was not a part of recognized NATO territory.

The enosis movement led, in the years 1958-59, to the most violent discussions in the Council between Greece and Turkey, which came to an end only when the Treaty of Zurich was signed in 1960. Under this treaty, Cyprus became independent; the constitution gave safeguards for Turkish minority rights, and this complex, over-all settlement was guaranteed by the United Kingdom, Greece, and Turkey, who obtained certain rights of intervention.

As far as we in NATO were aware, all went well until December, 1963.

At the NATO Ministerial Meeting in the beginning of December, 1963, I had a discussion with the ministers of foreign affairs of Turkey and Greece. I asked them whether they had any problems (besides their request for economic and military aid) on which I could help them. They assured me that there were no problems, that relations between Turkey and Greece had never been so good, and that they worked in perfect harmony—there was not a cloud in the sky!

Ten days later, Makarios (I am sure, acting on his own) renounced the Treaty and started his actions against the Turkish Cypriots.

Here I come to the subject of my paper: What should and could the Secretary General of NATO do under those circumstances? Cyprus was not NATO territory. From my readings in the history of Cyprus, I had received the impression that during all the vicissitudes of changing regimes that the island had known through the ages, there had always been one constant or stabilizing factor, the independent Cypriot Orthodox church, which had held its own against any odds. I had, furthermore, personally always been wary of treaties which grant so-called independence but reserve certain rights and give guarantees. In negotiations, Cyprus could have made a strong case and would have obtained sympathy from many sides. But the Greek Cypriots did not negotiate. They acted highhandedly, and often with great cruelty.

The only aspect of the problem at which NATO had to look was the impact of these actions on the relations between Greece and Turkey and on the solidarity and effectiveness of our southeastern flank. I knew how difficult it had been to bring some political and economic stability and some military strength to these two countries. Together the allies provided between 37 and 47 per cent of the defense budgets of Greece and Turkey, and more aid was needed. How could I help to provide this new aid when the two countries were using the aid that had been given to fight a hot or cold war among themselves?

From the beginning, in December, 1963, I feared the worst, and especially so when in the following months about forty thousand Turkish Cypriots had to leave their villages and settle as refugees in an area north of Nicosia under appalling conditions.

In the beginning, most member countries believed that no real crisis would arise. The United Kingdom hoped to solve the problem through its own diplomatic channels; the United States had too many serious problems of its own in the Far East; other nations, though keenly interested, applied a wait-and-see policy—while Greece gave direct support to the Greek Cypriots and Turkey prepared to invade the island.

I had the right and the duty to take some initiative if I came to the conclusion that the solidarity and effectiveness of the Alliance in the area were at stake. But how could I come to such a conclusion? The Secretary General has no political or diplomatic representatives of his own. He may hold in confidence information informally shown or given him by member countries, but he can never use this information as proof.

In December and January, I worked through military channels; and on the basis of information thus received, I sent notes to the two countries.

I am convinced that General Lemnitzer, at least once, and I, as Secretary General, probably twice, prevented, through our interventions, open hostilities. We have been extremely lucky that old Mr. Inonu of Turkey was willing to listen to our counsels; but every time we persuaded him

to contain his people, I must confess I had misgivings as
to whether we were not at the same time playing into the
hands of Makarios.

As time passed, the situation became more explosive.
The Security Council went into action. United Nations
forces were sent; a mediator was appointed. But in spite
of these measures, Makarios continued building up his
forces. The United Nations had too limited an authority
for effective intervention. I believed the situation so critical
that I decided to go personally to Athens and Ankara.
While Greece made this visit very difficult, the Turks were
forthright and co-operative. I also entered into useful contact with the Secretary General of the United Nations,
U Thant.

The May Ministers Meeting backed my efforts and gave
the Secretary General a watching brief; that is, I was to
follow the situation closely and consult the Council whenever I deemed it necessary.

It was only on a second visit to Greece and Turkey that
I succeeded—and then only by rather unorthodox means—
in having a long and frank discussion with the Greek government on the evening of my arrival. They agreed that
something had to be done; the "Natofication" of the island
through enosis was discussed, and we agreed that time had
to be gained for mediation by the United Nations, perhaps
through a double guarantee: one to Cyprus against invasion by Turkey, the other to the Turkish Cypriots afford-
ing them genuine protection. That same night I contacted
Washington. The next day Undersecretary of State George
Ball came to Athens and, after consultations with the
Greeks, went the day after on to Ankara, where I arrived
half a day later. Naturally, there was no immediate agree-

ment on the suggestions I had discussed with the Greek government, but at least the United States started to play a much more active role, which I considered essential to any solution, and Mr. Dean Acheson was shortly sent to Geneva to assist the UN mediator.

I felt at that time that there was some change in the attitude of the Greek government; perhaps Makarios' visit to Egypt and his contacts with Moscow jarred the Turks from their previous fatalism and the Greeks from their sense of the inevitability of a tragedy which had to take its course.

A solution has not yet been found, but perhaps the chances for negotiations have improved.

I have not, for reasons that, I am sure, you appreciate, gone into all the details of this difficult period; but I hope that this brief discussion will, at least, illustrate for you the possibilities for action in this type of difficulty, and the limitations placed on such actions on the part of the Secretary General. For what I am discussing is not the whole Cyprus issue, but rather the function and role of the Secretary General of NATO.

France and Its Diminishing Will to Co-operate

It would be interesting to describe the historical, psychological, and even the philosophical reasons for the diminishing will to co-operate with NATO of France under De Gaulle. This is, however, not my subject. Let me speak, therefore, only of my contacts as Secretary General with France and De Gaulle.

Before doing so, however, I must tell you my reasons for regarding France under De Gaulle as being no longer a full working member, but rather an associate member, of NATO. The French will to co-operate in NATO has practically disappeared; and we are presently faced with a series of rigid French positions in NATO, while the French are becoming increasingly isolated from the current development of the Atlantic Alliance.

Let me provide but a few examples: France under De Gaulle has withdrawn its Mediterranean and Atlantic fleets from NATO; has assigned only a small part of its air force to the integrated air defense of Europe; has assigned only a small part of its land forces to NATO (the figures for the army and air force are slightly over 60,000 men out of a total defense establishment of 690,000); has established within the Alliance an isolated position on strategy; has not allowed non-French nuclear weapons on French territory; has not participated in the studies for a Multilateral Force; has been the only country not to accept the 1963 Athens Guidelines for the use of the atomic bomb; has not participated in defense aid for Greece; has refused to sign the Nuclear Test Ban Treaty; has not participated, though a member, in the Eighteen Nations Disarmament Conference in Geneva; and has pursued—as is its right—its own policies on China, Vietnam, and Cyprus, but without any serious prior consultation with its NATO allies.

To this list should be added details on French positions in the NATO Council on split communiqués after ministerial meetings, and France's hostile attitude toward the International Secretariat and the Secretary General on basic questions of procedure and administration.

But before doing so, I must add one significant item; namely, that France under De Gaulle has withdrawn from its obligation to submit the level of its stocks of nuclear weapons to a majority decision of the Western European Union, as provided in the Protocol on the Control of Armaments of the Brussels Treaty of 1954. From this treaty obligation, France under De Gaulle has withdrawn itself. It should not be overlooked that it is this same treaty which controls German armament, and under which Germany renounced the production of atomic, biological, and chemical weapons in Germany.

Turning now to the relations of the Secretary General with the French government, I should first, by way of contrast, note what in my time these relations were with the United States government, for instance. During these years in which I was the Secretary General, I received every morning a briefing on United States foreign policy in different areas. Every year I went to Washington several times for meetings with the State Department, the Pentagon, and the White House. All these discussions were carefully prepared; and, when at the end of a visit the President received me, he had been briefed on the issues which would have to be submitted to him. Similar arrangements were always made in other capitals, but nothing of the kind ever happened in France. On the contrary, on taking office my initial request to pay my respects to De Gaulle went unanswered for three months. I then saw him for twenty-five minutes and never again, not even to pay a farewell call on my retirement. Prime Minister Debré I saw once for fifteen minutes; Prime Minister Pompidou, twice for twenty minutes; and Foreign Minister Couve de Murville, once for fifteen minutes. Only with the Minister of Defense, Messmer, did I have personal contact.

I do not cite these facts out of personal pique at what was clearly a rebuff by De Gaulle and his government. Personal pique does, certainly, play a role in international politics, but there is no place for it in the role of the Sec-

retary General of NATO. I cite these facts rather because
they are an important indication of the French attitude
toward NATO, and of the basic political limitations on what
the Secretary General, even with the best of will, can
achieve. Noting a diminishing French will to co-operate in
NATO, I realized that it was obviously the task of the
Secretary General to try to ascertain the reasons for this
development, and if possible, to retard or halt a development so negative in its implications for the Alliance. But
the Secretary General can only ascertain such reasons and,
above all, can only hope to influence such a development
by discussions with the men responsible for it—namely, the
responsible members of the French government. If they
exclude even the possibility of such discussions, it is, of
course, a significant measure of the inflexibility of their
attitudes and of the very limited degree to which they
consider allied relations open to negotiation on any but
their own terms. I could thus accomplish little in the way
of direct persuasion or discussion with the French, and the
resulting record is a sorry one.

During my tenure of office, France systematically tried to
minimize the function of the Secretary General and the
International Staff. France, for instance, vetoed for many
months a long overdue increase in salaries for the International Staff; vetoed the appointment of one man who
should be the responsible officer, under the Secretary General, for a work of more than $300 million on a new com-
munications system for modern airplanes; vetoed for a
long time the appointment of a science adviser; tried to
prevent the Secretary General from asking personal advice
on a military problem from SACEUR; refused for a long time
to explain to me or my staff its policy on strategy; and

permitted me only once or twice in more than three years
to read a French political report.

When I had come to the conclusion that this was the
system by which the French wanted to express their dis-
pleasure with the function of the Secretary General, I did
not ask for direct contact any longer, but found my own
ways to obtain the information I needed, showed endless
patience, and refused to be affected or disturbed by the
French attitude. In the end, the Council, for the most part,
obtained what it needed; but the waste of time and energy,
which could have been spent on so many other much more
important questions but which was required to deal with
the French attitude, was a high price to have to pay.

I have often wondered whether there was a personal
reason for this attitude. France delayed for at least three
months before it finally agreed to my appointment. Were
they opposed to a Dutchman in this job, or did they consider me to be a man without any understanding for, or
willingness to consider, their point of view?

In the beginning I regularly offered to give a report to
the French minister concerned after I had had important
discussions in Washington, London, or Bonn, but I was
never asked to do so. Finally, I gave up speculating and
just accepted this attitude as a fact of life.

My interview with President de Gaulle was an extraordinary experience. I was summoned, after three months,
to the Elysée Palace on short notice, just when I was to
take a plane for London. I did not know what De Gaulle
wanted to speak about. When I came into the room, he was
sitting behind a very large desk, and he asked me, in his
inimitable way, four very direct questions.

The first one was: "Mr. Stikker, do you expect that we
are going to have a war?"

This was in 1961. I replied, "It seems to me that there may be a change in Soviet policy; Khrushchev and his generals begin to understand the dangers of nuclear war, and if the West remains united, if we maintain our military strength, and if there is no scientific development which will change the existing balance of terror, then I am rather confident that we can maintain the peace."

De Gaulle's reaction to this remark was rather cool; he did not like my three "if's," and after having indicated, but not very clearly, that he based his policy on the thesis that there can be no war, certainly not a conventional one, he abruptly changed the subject and asked me, "Qu'est-ce que vous pensez du Président Kennedy?" ("What do you think of President Kennedy?")

I did not like this kind of direct and personal question and made quite a story around Mr. Kennedy, his desire for peace, his knowledge of history, his original thinking, his devotion to NATO, his senatorial experience, his human and direct contact, his careful study of subjects, the weighing of his words, and so I went on and on, until finally De Gaulle interrupted and brought my exposition to an end with the remark, "En tout cas, c'est un homme responsable." ("At any rate, he is a man of responsibility.")

Some years later, President Kennedy asked me the same question about De Gaulle. When I told him this story and came to the point where De Gaulle had said in French, "En tout cas, c'est un homme responsable," Kennedy interrupted (saying that his French was somewhat rusty) and asked, "Am I right in translating De Gaulle's remark as 'I may be an s.o.b., but in any case I am an s.o.b. with some kind of responsibility'?"

"Perhaps this translation is quite correct," I replied, 'but the remark has a deeper meaning also." For a few days after my interview with De Gaulle, I met Guy Mollet, now in the opposition but in 1958 one of De Gaulle's close collaborators in the Cabinet. I asked him to explain to me what the meaning of those rather flippant words, as I saw them then, of De Gaulle might be. Mollet found this remark by De Gaulle about Kennedy's "responsibility" most revealing. When in 1958 De Gaulle came back into power and Mollet helped him to draft the new constitution, De Gaulle had insisted that the ultimate responsibility for France in time of an internal or an external crisis should rest in the hands of the Président de la République and that there should be no doubt about this. This provision has now been laid down in Article 16 of the Constitution.

Guy Mollet explained to me that De Gaulle's desire for this power went back to May, 1940, when France was invaded by Hitler's armies and when at the most critical moment neither the president, nor the prime minister, nor Parliament could act, and there was only utter confusion arising from divided responsibility. De Gaulle had said, "Look at Holland; we were unable to act, but there in Holland Queen Wilhelmina, by leaving the country, took with her in her own hands the full responsibility for her country. That is what I want." He clearly admired the Constitution of the United States which gives the President this sole responsibility!

The third question De Gaulle asked me was whether I believed in the integration of military forces for the defense of Europe. I replied, "Undoubtedly, modern war or defense are no longer possible without integration."

De Gaulle disagreed and explained: "Since the insurrection in Algiers, I cannot rely on my generals and officers. That situation has to be changed, but loyalty can only be restored if the army and the officers know what they are fighting for, that is, for France; they cannot fight or be loyal to some philosophical concept like NATO, and they cannot be loyal to some unknown American general or admiral."

"But we are fighting for our joint freedom," I replied. "We can only remain free if we all join our forces. Separate efforts of the small countries, or of Germany, have no meaning. Besides—I do not believe that Eisenhower or Norstad are unknown generals."

De Gaulle disagreed: he wanted to be "independent" although he recognized that Norstad was "un bon soldat," "a good soldier."

The fourth question De Gaulle asked me was, "Do you really believe that the United States will ever use the bomb purely for the defense of Europe?"

"Yes," I replied, "and not only because they have repeatedly said so since the creation of NATO, but also because it is in the direct interest of the United States that Europe remain free."

De Gaulle did not agree. "They will use the bomb purely for their own interest; that is the reason why France must have a bomb of its own."

I then asked him, "When you have the bomb, will you then use it for Europe?"

"Just as the United States, I will use the bomb for our own interest," he replied.

I had learned a lot in this brief interview about De Gaulle's convictions and desire for "independence" and "responsibility," but the example of this interview makes it clear how complicated the job of Secretary General can be.

Strategy and the Secretary General

Several years ago, General Norstad was asked in a public meeting of parliamentarians, "What is the reason that there is not more standardization in weaponry, or unity in strategic thinking?"

He replied, "There are three reasons or obstacles: the first is the United States, the second is the United Kingdom, and the third is France."

That answer was then quite correct, but now we should, I believe, add at least two more reasons: Germany and Italy.

Bringing these five reasons under one common denominator—growing nationalism—and looking for ways to combat this trend, we come back once again to: the will to co-operate, not to adopt rigid positions, not to give way to pressure groups or political prejudices—plainly, to give priority to unity. This unity is what to my mind the Secretary General stands for and must fight for.

The sources of information for the Secretary General in the military field are rather insufficient; he has no military adviser and the Standing Group and Military Committee do not inform him fully about what they are doing. It was nevertheless possible for me, through documentation by the civilian staff and through personal study and frequent personal contacts, to acquire sufficient knowledge on strategic issues to do my job. I believed that, since the Secretary General has the right of initiative, he should try to help the Council to overcome these five obstacles and to maintain our unity. Strategy, as we all know, is not just a philosophy. In order to develop a strategy, we have to start with an assessment of the threat; we then have to look at the geography and the history of the area concerned; we must know whether we act alone or jointly with allies;

we must know the will of the countries who are our allies to fight and defend themselves, the weapons which are needed, and the resources in money and manpower which can be made available.

The threat assessment is constantly under review, and I think that it can be said objectively that present NATO strategy is based de facto on three principles: *flexibility*— meaning that NATO must have the capability to respond to any kind of attack with the appropriate means; a *forward concept*—which means simply that defense in Europe should be as near to the borders of NATO territories as possible; and *integration* of the armed forces of the member countries. The question is to what extent do the five countries—the five "obstacles"—have their own differing ideas about this de facto situation.

The United States agrees with this strategy in principle, but believes that, in order to make it effective, the appropriate military means available to the Alliance, especially in the conventional field, should be increased by say, 20 per cent in Europe. The United Kingdom fears too much flexibility, probably because it does not believe it has the capability to increase its own defense efforts. France disagrees with each of the three principles.

In the French view a war in Europe which would be fought with only conventional weapons or tactical atomic weapons must lead to disaster. Instead of flexibility, France, therefore, favors a "trip-wire" strategy, under which any attack in Europe going beyond a certain line will be met by an immediate response with strategic nuclear weapons. The French believe that this is the only strategy which will act as an effective deterrent to war.

France's assignment of something less than 10 per cent of its military effectives to NATO, while the remainder are to be deployed for the defense of France and French interests, implies that France has accepted a "backward" rather than a forward strategy.

As for integration, France under De Gaulle has made no secret of its opposition. Under present French policy, if there is to be a war, France wants to fight its war with its forces for the defense of its territories under the command of its officers directed by its president. It is, as I said, a vital provision of the Constitution of the Fifth Republic, insisted upon by De Gaulle in 1958, that the president be vested with full responsibility.

Germany is steadily building up its conventional strength, could probably do even more, but is worried about its lack of any real participation in the responsibility for nuclear weapons and is apprehensive about a possible withdrawal of United States forces from Europe.

Italy is not doing badly, but while it would like to increase its status as a medium large country through some participation in nuclear-weapons strategy, it has great domestic problems that render an immediate increase in defense effort or participation in MLF extremely difficult at this moment.

To this list of obstacles should be added Greece and Turkey, both already spending too much on defense and aware that geographically they cannot cope with a conventional invasion and both, therefore, as far as the southeastern flank of NATO is concerned, opposed to any system of flexibility.

When as Secretary General I had made for myself this analysis of the situation, I began, under my right of initiative, to suggest to the Council that we should not continue discussions on the basis of the theoretical approach represented by the rewriting of the old political directive which the Council had given in 1956 to military authorities. We should look instead at our practical problems and move ahead step by step.

The first step was in the nuclear field. Ministers there accepted certain steps forward. The United States gave guarantees and information; some European officers were stationed at SAC; a deputy for nuclear weapons under SACEUR was appointed; British Bomber Command was assigned to SACEUR; Polaris submarines were assigned to SACEUR and are in European waters; and systems for consultation on the use of nuclear weapons anywhere in the world were developed. These measures certainly represent progress, but grave problems still have to be solved.

As total disarmament should be our ultimate aim, the proliferation of nuclear weapons should be prevented. Now there are five nuclear powers; each new member of the nuclear club practically doubles the dangers and stirs the ambition of others to follow. In all my efforts to make NATO members unite in an agreed policy on the availability and use of nuclear weapons, I, as Secretary General, hoped that we could develop a system under which Europe could share as a partner in the decision on NATO-assigned weapons, and that no members other than the United States, the United Kingdom and France should have their own weapons over which they had individual power of decision. The possession of these weapons by the United Kingdom and France is, to my mind, of secondary importance because the use of these weapons without simultaneous United States action would make no sense and is therefore highly improbable. But further proliferation in Europe would certainly start off a chain of serious political reactions. Germany does not, in my opinion, desire to have a bomb of its own, and I am equally convinced that France is not willing to give it to her.

I must say some words in this connection about the Multilateral Nuclear Force (MLF). The MLF has received so much publicity that many people consider it a problem which stands by itself. *It does not.* MLF is only part of an over-all nuclear arrangement which has to be established between the United States and the other NATO members for the defense of Europe. There is needed (and this, again, concerns strategy) a specific number of strategic nuclear weapons. These can be provided partly by the MLF, but also by the British Bomber Command, by the Polaris submarines of the United States and the United Kingdom, by a relatively small number of weapons from SAC, and, finally, by the already available weapons in Europe under bilateral agreement.

Once we accept the principle that an arrangement, military and political, has to be found for all these weapons-systems, which by their very nature involve different forms of participation by the various members of NATO, a solution can, to my mind, be found. I do not exclude the possibility even of finding a system of co-operation (perhaps a better word is "co-ordination") with the French nuclear striking force, the *force de frappe.*

The other step for the development of a new strategy concerned the conventional means for implementing that strategy. The International Staff had, at my request, made an initial study of what it would mean to increase, for example, the European conventional forces by 20 per cent. We came to the conclusion that such an increase as an over-all figure would be utterly impossible for economic and political reasons, and that the manpower is just not available.

The result of these studies was quite surprising to me. We found, for instance, that the quality and cost of American forces is so different from European standards that in dollars the total cost of the existing seventy-three M-day and first echelon divisions in Europe was half of the total cost of the twenty-five American divisions in the same categories. We also found that while the per capita income of the population in Europe is about half of that in the United States, the percentage of the gross national products which goes into government revenues is higher in Europe than in the United States. An easy solution for a very substantial increase in European conventional weapons is, therefore, not in the cards. Much more careful study, in conjunction with member countries and military authorities, of the relationship between strategy, military requirements, and available resources has to be made.

After many months of personal discussions between the Secretary General and several member countries, the Council of Ministers finally decided that this confrontation to attempt reconciliation of strategy, requirements, and resources should take place. After many difficulties with France (especially after NATO military authorities, who went their own way in looking for a theoretical solution, had arrived at a complete deadlock), these studies are now under way. It was largely due to some discussions with French Minister of Defense Messmer, in the presence of French Chief of Staff Ailleret, that progress could be made.

All this was what I, as Secretary General, was working for when I was obliged to retire. The Atlantic Alliance is strong but is still in difficulty. An over-all settlement of the nuclear problem, an agreed level of conventional forces, can contribute to the development of a new strategy that means a new political directive.

This would bring about new unity; it would create an atmosphere of tranquillity and balance in Western relations, so that we all could concentrate on how to create a Europe capable of working with the United States in an Atlantic partnership to preserve the peace against any odds, and spend more of our resources on fighting the battle against poverty and ignorance and on helping the underdeveloped.

To contribute to these high aims was the task of the Secretary General as I saw it.

Cortlandt V. R. Schuyler

Military Defense in the Western Alliance

THE PROBLEMS confronting the NATO Alliance today are both
political and military in nature. It is impossible to separate
entirely one category from the other. However, in this discussion, I shall endeavor to focus primarily on the military
aspects of these matters, straying into the political field
only where this becomes necessary for a full understanding
of the NATO military role.

As a planner in the Pentagon, I was closely associated
with the parents while our first NATO child was a-borning.
A year or so later, I was in on the arrival of the second
NATO baby. This time I was in Paris with General Eisenhower's original planning group, where we gave birth to
Supreme Headquarters Allied Powers Europe, known there-
after as SHAPE. Except for a brief interval spent in com-

manding a division in Germany, I remained with this child for the next nine years, a time-record, if that means anything, surpassed only by that of General Norstad. Thus I helped guide our infant through its numerous childhood crises, and since retirement in 1959, I have watched with great interest its adolescent struggles and the maturing of many of our earlier programs.

Of course, since my discussion will deal primarily with these NATO children's future, not their past, all this is of only secondary interest. But it is appropriate, I think, to dwell very briefly at this point on what NATO has already accomplished. This is not just to indulge an old soldier's whim to talk about bygone days, but rather an effort to provide a framework for a clear understanding of the influences and pressures which today are threatening to disrupt the very foundations of the NATO structure.

NATO was created primarily, though not entirely, as a military alliance. The late 1940's had witnessed the enslavement under Soviet communism of the peoples of one nation after another in eastern Europe and the Balkans. Our earlier postwar dreams of establishing democratic, freely elected regimes throughout these areas had gone glimmering. We watched with growing consternation as the vast Soviet armies, refusing to withdraw when the fighting was over, took over full control of eastern Europe and executed or expelled to Siberia all national leaders who refused to co-operate. They thus paved the way for puppet governments which, when created, proceeded ruthlessly with the extermination of the last remnants of Western democratic influences and with the imposition of communist regimes in the Soviet pattern on cowed and dispirited peoples.

In western Europe, the impact of all this was not slow in coming. With the Soviet armies poised less than one hundred miles from the Rhine, with local communist parties increasing in power, with national economies weakened by the war, unemployment still high, and national military strength almost non-existent, the burning question in every nation was not, "Will the Soviets overrun us, too?" but rather, "How soon will they arrive?" To say the least, confidence in western Europe's future in true freedom was at an all-time low.

This was the critical situation in early 1947 which the United States sought to redress, first by an extensive and military aid program to Greece and Turkey, second through the Marshall Plan. But the loss of Czechoslovakia through a communist coup in February of 1948 was a clear indication that something even more tangible in the way of outside support would have to be forthcoming if western Europe was to weather the storm. Fortunately, that "something" was already under way, sparked by Winston Churchill's speech at Fulton, Missouri, in 1946, and by the Vandenburg Resolution of June, 1948. Accordingly, in July negotiations for a defensive alliance got under way in Washington, leading in April, 1949, to the signing by twelve member nations (later increased to fifteen) of the North Atlantic Treaty. The Treaty provided generally for economic and cultural collaboration among the members, but its key provision was the specific agreement that an attack on any one of them would be considered an attack on all and that necessary assistance would be provided accordingly.

The Treaty established at top level a North Atlantic Council, on which each member state was given representation. The Council held its first meeting in Washington in September, 1949, and proceeded at once with the business of setting up staff and planning committees to deal with the most urgent military and political problems.

But in June, 1950, the forces of North Korea—equipped, trained and directed by the Soviets—attacked the lightly armed South Koreans and quickly overran most of their territory. This event had a profound effect on the nations of western Europe. It was proof, in fact, that no mere paper treaty could save them from a similar fate unless they could also establish a common military defense *in being*, able to meet any invasion at their borders. Their response was the selection by the NATO Council of General Eisenhower as NATO's Supreme Commander Europe, and the establishment, in April, 1951, just outside Paris, of his Supreme Headquarters Allied Powers Europe (SHAPE). Except for certain designated naval and territorial defense units, all the forces of all the member states in the European area were assigned to his command. Somewhat later, a Supreme Allied Commander Atlantic (SACLANT), also an American, was appointed, with headquarters at Norfolk, Virginia, where they have remained to this day, in command of the naval forces of the Alliance in the North Atlantic area.

Directly under the Atlantic Council, on the military side, there was established a Defense Committee, which after the first year or two was replaced by a NATO Military Committee consisting of the top military officer of each NATO government. The chairman of the Joint Chiefs of Staff has been, and still is, the United States member. But because these key officers are busy in their own capitals, the Military Committee has, unfortunately, met infrequently. Its operational task, as well as its staff work, has been delegated to a Standing Group of three top-ranking officers, one each from France, Great Britain, and the United States. The Military Committee and its Standing Group are the Council's military advisers, and they provide, with the Council's general blessing, strategic and operational guidance to the two supreme commanders.

This, in broad outline, is NATO's military organizational structure; it has endured, in generally the same form, to this day. SHAPE, NATO's top European command, is a fully integrated—or mix-manned, if you prefer the term—headquarters, of four hundred odd officers, drawn from thirteen of the fifteen member states. Portugal, with no troops assigned, maintains only a liaison officer at SHAPE, and Iceland, having no military establishment, is not represented.

Scattered about Europe from Norway to Turkey, all subordinate to SHAPE, are some twenty odd similar, but smaller, NATO headquarters, each organized and integrated in the SHAPE pattern, to which are assigned the various national army, navy, and air forces, including those of the United States. The entire complex is supported by an integrated pipeline system carrying gasoline and oil, a NATO-constructed system of several hundred airfields, a combined communications network, and an integrated, fully manned chain of early-warning radar stations. Thus, while the NATO forces themselves remain national in character, their command system and much of their logistic support is, and has been for some years, fully integrated on a NATO-wide basis. This arrangement has insured full participation by all members in NATO's military plans and operations.

The purpose underlying NATO's military buildup has remained unchanged since its inception. It is twofold: first, to establish and maintain a force structure so constituted and so deployed as to render aggression in any form— limited or all-out—unprofitable for a would-be attacker;

in other words, to *deter* any and all types of aggression. And, second, to create a feeling of confidence among NATO peoples that the future security of their territories can and will be preserved.

The situation in western Europe today attests to the success of this considerable effort. Military strength, in being, exists. Economies are booming. Governments are stable. And despite communist successes in other parts of the world, the surging Soviet tide of the 1940's in Europe has been stopped in its tracks. True, NATO's forces have not even yet reached the goals recommended by the Military Committee and approved by the Council. Nevertheless, NATO's military strength in 1965 is four or five times what it was in 1950. And the likelihood of Soviet aggression is probably less than at any time since the Alliance was created.

Any purely numerical comparison of NATO ground strength with that of the Eastern bloc is difficult, and perhaps not too meaningful. Questions of relative effectiveness, of terrain conditions, of logistic support—all these factors must be considered also. In Central Europe, NATO's twenty-six or twenty-seven divisions are matched by approximately an equal number of Soviet divisions, deployed in the satellite areas. The satellites themselves can muster some sixty divisions, but in an attack on the West, many, perhaps most of these, would be needed to maintain order in their own countries and to guard the thousands of miles of supply line leading from the interior of Russia.

On balance, it seems reasonable to conclude that, with present deployment, any Soviet surprise attack with conventional ground forces could probably be stopped before it reached the Rhine. Of course, in preparation for an attack, the Soviets could greatly augment their forward strength to a level which NATO could not possibly match. But a buildup of this nature would indicate preparation for a major war, probably global in character.

Relative strengths of conventional air forces are even more difficult to assess. With present deployments, the balance is probably in NATO's favor. But there are hundreds of airfields in the satellite countries, and the Soviets could, perhaps, in a few weeks achieve a massive concentration of air-support forces by moving units from the interior of Russia and from elsewhere. Here again, however, such a buildup would signal preparations for a global conflict.

Thus NATO conventional strength in Central Europe today represents the bare minimum needed to deal with any limited, surprise attack. If the thirty-division goal could be reached, a more satisfactory margin of safety would exist. Even thirty divisions, however, provide no guarantee of security against a major conventional attack preceded by an extended buildup of Soviet bloc ground and air strength. But the really important point in all this is that NATO's conventional forces and deployments *do* provide an effective deterrent against surprise attack.

This brings us to a consideration of NATO's nuclear power. From the very first, our prime deterrent against all-out Soviet attack has been, not NATO's forces in Europe, but rather the nuclear power of the United States. That power has been and will continue to be sufficient virtually to destroy Russia, if—God forbid!—we should ever be faced with the horror of global war. In addition, over the past eight or nine years, the United States has been embarked on a program of equipping NATO's European forces with so-called tactical or battlefield nuclear weapons—bombs deliverable by fighter-bombers and a wide variety of ground weapons delivered by mobile rocket-launchers and missile-launchers with ranges up to six or seven hundred miles, perhaps even a bit more. Allied units, which are made up of, among others, French, German, Belgian, Dutch, British, Italian, and, in some cases, Greek and Turkish troops, have been furnished planes and launchers; but nuclear warheads are stored in forward areas strictly under United States control. They can be released for actual use only by authority of the President of the United States, who, of course, similarly controls all such weapons in the hands of United States forces. Thus, except for a relatively few weapons of British and, more recently, French manufacture, the President himself controls the employment of NATO's entire nuclear arsenal. However, the United States has an explicit understanding with each allied nation that no nuclear weapon can be launched from the soil of the "host" country until the specific agreement of the host has been obtained.

It should be noted, however, that these restrictions on employment of nuclear weapons, complicated as they may seem, do not involve significant *operational* delays. The weapons themselves are stored at airfields and launching sites, close by the delivery vehicles. Personnel are highly trained in quick-loading techniques. Communications are provided so that a "release" order, once it is given by the President, can be transmitted to field commanders almost in a matter of seconds. And allied nuclear-trained units would be able to execute the order with almost the same rapidity as would their American counterparts.

Over the year, of course, Soviet nuclear missile strength has similarly increased. The U.S.S.R. now has some two hundred IRBM's capable of reaching any part of the United States. But what is more important to the Europeans, there are today in the areas of western Russia and the satellite countries, hundreds, perhaps thousands, of mobile Soviet missiles capable of destroying airfields, supply installations, and even cities throughout western Europe. This point is important to keep in mind in discussing strategies for the defense of Europe.

Despite NATO's unblemished record of past success, however, no one would deny that the Alliance today is in serious trouble. This trouble centers, not on any reassessment of NATO's defensive purpose—deterrence of aggression and assurance of future security—for, quite obviously, there is no disagreement here. Rather, the burning question is whether or not, in this changing world of the 1960's, some new strategy, some basic alterations in NATO's military structure, perhaps even a revision of the Treaty itself, is required. Of course, General de Gaulle is the chief proponent of change. But he does not stand entirely alone. While few, if any, of NATO's other leaders support all his arguments, there are, nevertheless, those who feel that certain changes are long overdue.

Let us, then, attempt to examine the De Gaulle thesis. This is not easy, primarily because nowhere can we yet find a De Gaulle blueprint for the future. That is not his style. Emmet Hughes, in *Newsweek*, recently quoted an unnamed De Gaulle aide as saying, "I don't truly know what his European policy is, and I'm not wholly sure he does either." But through a study of his writings and speeches and by considering his actions in a variety of instances, the general trend of his thinking is becoming clear.

The fundamental element in the De Gaulle concept is his basic concern regarding what he considers to be the growing Anglo-American dominance in NATO affairs. This attitude stems perhaps from his wartime experience, and it has not altered significantly over the years. He accepts the fact that during the postwar period of Europe's recovery, American aid and American military guidance were essential. But now that Europe is back on her feet, he believes very sincerely that the time has come for her to work out her own destiny politically, economically, and militarily. He seems to feel that NATO, under present plans and policies, inhibits rather than helps progress toward this goal. Entirely aside from the NATO Alliance, he appears to visualize a future loose association of fully sovereign European states held together by common interests and guided, of course, largely by France. He would prefer to see the United States in the role of a friendly overseas colleague, rather than as a coparticipant in Europe's affairs. And he appears to seek retention of the United States guarantee of nuclear assistance in an emergency, but only if and when Europe *by itself* calls for that assistance. Within this context, De Gaulle's attitudes on a wide variety of NATO problems are certainly understandable. In the nuclear field, for example, as far back as 1958, De Gaulle proposed to the President and the British Prime Minister a NATO *directoire* of French, British and American representatives for the purpose of formulating nuclear and general strategy for the Alliance and, indeed, planning operations of the three nations on a world-wide basis. He made the point that the military employment of a nuclear weapon *anywhere* could trigger a global war and that, therefore, France's voice should be heard in the decision to use it. Essentially, this sort of arrangement would have given the French a veto over any United States employment of its nuclear strength. Moreover, it was apparent that the other NATO members could never accept this "inner circle" domination of NATO's major plans and policies. Accordingly, the proposal was rejected. Thereupon, De

Gaulle undertook to augment very considerably the resources and effort devoted to his own atomic weapons program. This has culminated in the development of the French *force de frappe,* a force which the General refuses to allocate to NATO. Rather he insists on retaining it in its full national status under his direct control.

In American eyes, these French efforts constitute an unnecessary diversion of very significant economic and scientific resources. Even at its peak, De Gaulle's force will represent less than 5 per cent of NATO's nuclear power, and that small addition has no strategic justification. The French are, of course, still years behind in nuclear technology. And as they endeavor to progress from atom to hydrogen bombs, from bombs to missiles, from relatively simple to highly complex and sophisticated control and guidance systems, research and development difficulties will multiply, costs will mount astronomically, and other portions of their military program will suffer correspondingly. In fact, it is likely that for years to come, the *force de frappe* will continue as a symbol of French prestige rather than as a meaningful strategic asset.

In 1958, De Gaulle informed General Norstad, then SHAPE's Supreme Commander, that he could no longer permit the stockage on French soil of nuclear warheads unless they were placed under strict French control. Any such arrangement, even if desirable, could not have been sanctioned by United States law, and General Norstad accordingly found it necessary to move the American air squadrons, with their nuclear weapons, from their locations in France to air fields in other NATO areas.

De Gaulle is not in sympathy with the present NATO organization of "integrated" headquarters and support facilities. Not only does he feel that French officers have been bypassed in the selection of major NATO commanders, but he is also fundamentally opposed to any form of integration, feeling that it diminishes the stature of *national* staffs and commands. The French Minister of Defense, Pierre Messmer, has suggested that the entire NATO integrated command system could well be abolished and replaced by an arrangement for planning co-ordination among member states, through a group of joint international committees. Such a move, inconceivable today to France's partners, would nullify years of progress, destroy the allied potential for rapid military action, and seriously weaken the credibility of the NATO deterrent.

Of course, De Gaulle has far too keen a military understanding not to recognize these dangers. However, he appears ready to accept risks involved in the interest of freeing European forces from the fetters which bind them to the NATO command system, thus better preparing them for a later regrouping within his future European Association. At any rate, perhaps in an effort to set the pattern, he has step by step, over several years, withdrawn from their NATO command assignments all French naval units as well as major elements of the army and air force. Today, only the two French divisions in Germany, with their air support, remain assigned to NATO.

Nevertheless, General de Gaulle has frequently denied that he is basically anti-NATO. (And there is, indeed, no reason to believe he is.) He appears to recognize fully the present utility of the Alliance, but he would like to see it remodeled so that it will not constitute a stumbling block to his objectives. In the Khrushchev-induced Berlin crisis of 1961, De Gaulle was among the first to insist on a firm NATO stand against any concessions to the Soviets. His

representatives at that time played their full role in planning
for a variety of possible military actions, and he made it
clear that he was prepared to participate in the use of force,
if necessary, to maintain our right of entry to Berlin, both
by land and by air. He stood firmly behind President Kennedy in the latter's forthright action in the Cuban crisis,
making it clear to our representative that *had* he (De
Gaulle) been in the President's place, *he* would have taken
a similar course. All this, however, cannot hide the fact
that there are today wide areas of disagreement between
France and the United States concerning NATO policies and
structures.

There is another serious problem confronting the Alliance today: what one writer has called NATO's Great Nuclear Schism, the question of control and direction of
NATO's nuclear power. The fact is, of course, that a number
of our European friends are unhappy in feeling—whether
they are justified or not—that, under present arrangements,
they themselves will play a very minor role in the great
crisis decision on the employment of nuclear weapons.
And yet they have thus far failed entirely to agree on any
workable full-partnership proposal. A partial solution, the
MLF, has been put forward by the United States. Let us look
at it for a moment.

Though first suggested four or five years ago, the concept received its true initial impetus at the Kennedy-Mac-
millan Bahamas conference in 1962. The cancellation at
that time of the U.S. Skybolt project, which would have
equipped British bombers with the very latest in nuclear
missiles, had been a serious blow to the British Conserva-
tive government. It presaged the ultimate disappearance

of Britain as a nuclear power. To ease the situation, the United States conferees put forward a proposal for a two-pronged NATO nuclear force. One prong was to consist of national nuclear units, committed unreservedly to NATO by the British and French. The British would contribute their V-bombers and three to five Polaris-type submarines, which the United States would help them to equip. The French contribution was to be General de Gaulle's *force de frappe.*

The second prong was to be a mix-manned nuclear naval force of twenty to twenty-five surface ships equipped with Polaris-type nuclear missiles. Crews would be drawn from all participating NATO nations. The United States would retain control of the warheads, at least until Congress might decree otherwise, but all participants would, of course, hold a veto over their use.

General de Gaulle, consulted later, refused to join in any contribution of national forces, and that aspect of the proposal was accordingly dropped. But the United States has continued to press for adoption of the mix-manned force concept, the MLF. Arguments in its favor include the point that it meets in large part the requirement for Europe-based nuclear weapons to replace those now stored on NATO airfields, which have, as I pointed out, become vulnerable to Soviet surprise attack. More importantly, it is argued, participation in the force on the part of Germany and, perhaps, of other nations should satisfy their nuclear aspirations and thus avoid any further proliferation of independent nuclear powers.

Our own military leaders were initially somewhat cool to the concept. Later, however, perhaps under pressure from the White House, they have agreed that the idea is militarily feasible. A U.S. destroyer with mix-manned crew is now undergoing test operations.

European reactions have been mixed. The Belgians are uninterested; the Dutch hesitant. The Germans, at first enthusiastic, have more lately been holding back perhaps in deference to the French opposition. The Italians, Greeks, and Turks have at times shown interest, but obviously they would have great difficulty in paying their own way. The Norwegians and Danes want no part of it. The British Labor Government, after much soul-searching, has proposed broadening the concept to comprise what they have termed an Allied Nuclear Force (ANF). Their contribution would be, primarily, their three to five Polaris submarines, now being built, and their bomber force, all of which they would agree never to withdraw for national purposes; and they would expect NATO to pick up a good portion of the tab covering the cost of the submarine-construction program. They hope, of course, later to entice the French *force de force* into the structure, thus reverting, in effect, to the first prong of the original Bahamas proposal. On the mix-manned feature, they remain somewhat equivocal.

The French position is of particular interest. Initially, General de Gaulle seemed somewhat indifferent, so long as it was clearly understood that there would be no French participation. More recently, however, he has denounced the project in the strongest of terms. Prime Minister Pompidou has called it "provocative for France . . . and destructive for Europe." And De Gaulle himself, speaking at Strasburg, has said in referring to the Common Market nations in general—but with pointed reference to Germany and the MLF: "For one or another of these nations of the

European Economic Community in fact to renounce this union, at the cost of playing an auxiliary role, to yield over its fate to a power friendly indeed, but a power situated in a different world and whose destiny, by nature, and by history, could not be identified with that of Europe, . . . this would be to inflict a grievous wound upon a great hope." This one sentence makes it abundantly clear that MLF or any other proposed arrangement that promises to strengthen military, political, or economic ties between the United States and a Continental European nation or group of nations will find the General in vociferous opposition.

Fortunately, at the NATO full-dress Council meeting in Paris in December, 1964, the United States did not press for action and thus a head-on clash with France was avoided. Instead, the nations that are still interested—they now seem to be five: the United States, Great Britain, the Netherlands, Germany, and Italy—will discuss the proposal further at a separate meeting of their own in the near future.

Actually, it seems to some of us that U.S. advocates of the MLF have, in their enthusiasm, somewhat exaggerated the benefits they expect to see result from the concept. True, if MLF is created, it will produce some two hundred more nuclear missiles, with a European veto on their use. But if the United States continues to control the warheads, as seems likely, there can be no affirmative *European* decision on their employment. Instead, the situation will be analogous to that of the thousands of smaller nuclear weapons already in Europe, stockpiled for the various Allied national tactical units and available to them only when released by the President. Thus, there seems to be considerable doubt that MLF, offering the Europeans only a negative form of nuclear control, would in fact satisfy the

aspirations to become nuclear powers in their own right—
if these should develop—of nations like Germany or Italy.
More importantly, even with MLF in operation, Europe's
desire to be a full partner in the ultimate nuclear decision
would still not be realized. For 90 to 95 per cent of NATO's
nuclear support would still remain responsive solely to
Presidential action, with no possible European veto on that
decision. Thus MLF, though no doubt of some value both
militarily and politically, is hardly a revolutionary concept
for allied sharing of NATO nuclear power, as it has sometimes been claimed to be.

Under present conditions, the problem of sharing fully
in the ultimate decision on the use of nuclear weapons
literally defies solution. All agree that in a crisis, you can't
have fifteen fingers on the main nuclear trigger, fifteen
possible vetoes on its use. General Norstad has proposed
reducing the fifteen to five through an agreement that
would give the power of decision on *all* NATO weapons to a
five-nation committee which would include the three major
nations—Great Britain, France, and the United States—
with two others selected possibly on a rotating basis. But
he has generated little enthusiasm, even in this country,
for the idea. No nation, in peace, seems willing *de jure* to
delegate this critical decision to another.

Actually, we have been considering here only one part
of what is really a far broader dilemma—the entire question of how the Alliance can decide quickly to go to war.
On the other hand, a surprise attack, with either conventional or nuclear weapons, will require an immediate and
forceful *military* response. With perhaps the future survival of the Western World at stake, the nature and timing
of this response is in the first instance a political, not a
military, decision. On the other hand, in this Alliance of

fifteen independently sovereign nations, no political machinery has yet been devised to permit a decision of this magnitude to be made quickly. Each member state has its own laws governing its parliamentary and executive procedures, some of them approaching the archaic when it comes to dealing with the realities of the 1960's. But positive political decisions by the Alliance are largely the products of these various complex *national* decisions. Thus formal action by the NATO Council in a crisis might well not be forthcoming with the speed which the exigencies of the military situation would require. This is a problem which no juggling of NATO's military structure, no assignment of increased power to supreme commanders, can properly resolve. Under the circumstances, it is desirable, indeed essential, to continue the present *de facto* arrangement whereby the vast bulk of NATO's nuclear power can be released if necessary by action of the President.

The final answer must probably await the development of some form of Supreme European Authority able to act for its member states in vital matters of war and peace. At that time, the fifteen fingers on the nuclear—or the conventional—trigger might be reduced to two or three, but that day is a long way off.

In the meanwhile, a number of alleviating military measures can be taken. Some are already in process. In point of fact, even under today's arrangements, the fateful Presidential decision will never be taken without a considerable degree of allied participation. It will not come out of the blue, but only after numerous analyses and evaluations at lower levels, lesser decisions made as the crisis deepens. The NATO Council is already equipped to play a vital role here. On the military side, General Lemnitzer—now commanding at SHAPE—whose recommendations will be of first importance to the President, has recently been given a new nuclear deputy, a Belgian general, whose sole job it is to advise on nuclear planning and employment. And a group of European officers is now stationed at SAC headquarters in Omaha, to assist in all planning for nuclear operations in Europe. Even more can and no doubt will be done to give Europeans a still more important nuclear role in precrisis planning and operations.

Only General de Gaulle has developed a present solution to this nuclear problem—a solution which satisfies no one but himself. His solution is his nuclear *force de frappe,* held under his own *national* control. This arrangement permits him, on his own decision, to trigger off a nuclear exchange. And such action, once under way, could hardly fail but involve the entire nuclear strength of the United States and of the Alliance. Small wonder it fails to appeal to any of his allies!

And now bearing in mind the various points thus far discussed, we are forced to conclude that NATO's military situation today is both confusing and complicated. On the one hand, NATO forces in 1965 are stronger, and better trained and equipped than ever before. The command system is thoroughly organized and functioning effectively. At the moment, danger of external aggression seems minimal. No one can foresee what new threats future changes in Soviet policy may produce, but today East-West tensions are certainly at a low point.

On the other hand, paradoxically enough, never before in NATO's history has the future of the Alliance been so beclouded by uncertainties. There is the danger of nuclear proliferation, a danger which the United States seeks to avert through its MLF proposal. There are frustrations in

Europe over the continuing failure to solve to their satis-
faction the problem of nuclear control. There are deep
differences of opinion over strategy. And there are the
fast-developing French pressures for basic and far-reaching
changes in the organizational structure.

Although none of these problems lend themselves to
quick and easy solutions, they would not *by themselves,*
even all together, constitute a serious threat to NATO's future. But, unfortunately, they are the symptoms, not the
cause, of the malaise from which the Alliance is already
suffering and which could well reach crisis proportions
within the next year or two. For that cause we must, as
we have noted, look deeper: it stems from fundamentally
divergent views among the member nations as to Europe's
future and the role of the United States in it. Until that
crisis is resolved, or has run its course, it could well be
counter-productive to attempt to reach long-lasting solutions to peripheral military problems which cannot in
themselves contribute to a solution of the basic issue.

Rather, it would seem in the best interests of the Alliance and of all members concerned to alter NATO's *military*
policies and organization only to the extent absolutely
necessary to hold the Alliance together, leaving to some
future date any changes, desirable as they may be, which,
if adopted prematurely, might exacerbate present fundamental *political* disagreements.

After all, there is a great deal upon which all can agree.
NATO has served us well for fifteen years. It is just as essential for the future, as in the past, that we maintain a
solid front against aggression. Surely we can have faith
that, so long as the communist threat continues, the leaders of our Western nations will not damage, irreparably,
the Free World's most important bulwark.

Richard Goold-Adams

Political Co-operation in NATO

ALTHOUGH we still have four years to go before the initial twenty-year period of the North Atlantic Treaty is over, when it becomes legally and constitutionally possible for any country to give one year's notice to withdraw, I think that it is now, rather than in perhaps two or three years time, that the most critical stage has been reached. President Johnson has preferred to call this a period of change, rather than a crisis. If so, I would only add that it is a period of a revolutionary change in the relationships within the Alliance. The question is not just one of reforming the existing machinery for operating the Alliance. There are today, I believe, deeper divisions and greater divergencies between the nations composing the Alliance than at any previous time since the treaty was signed in 1949. I feel,

therefore, that my function is to outline why this is so; to
indicate to some degree what has been done in the past
to try to meet this kind of situation; and thus to suggest
how far we can draw on the lessons of the past in meeting
the problems of the future.

I shall start, first of all, by talking about some of the
functions of the Atlantic Council, dealing with some of the
thoughts and ideas that have been put forward from time
to time for making it more effective and perhaps adding
to its sphere of operations. Although a good many people
may be familiar with these ideas, it is necessary to summarize them in order to appreciate some of the difficulties
under which all political co-operation in NATO in fact takes
place.

As you probably know, under Article 2 of the North
Atlantic Treaty there is a provision whereby there should
be a certain degree of political and economic integration
within the Alliance. There has always been a great deal of
talk about this article, but very little action. I think perhaps
the most important moment in the discussion was back in
December, 1955, when a resolution of the Atlantic Council
led to the appointment of a special investigating commission, consisting of three foreign ministers, who became
known as the Three Wise Men: Mr. Pearson of Canada, Mr.
Lange of Norway, and Signor Martino of Italy. During
1956, they drew up a most trenchant report, which is still
the best commentary on the internal structure of NATO from
a political point of view. This report led in effect to the
Council's meeting more often, to its discussing a wider
range of subjects, and to its being treated with more confidence by the major powers. And my own view is that,
as a result of what happened in the years immediately

afterward, the Atlantic Council some time ago reached its maximum efficiency and its maximum usefulness. Hence I feel that any suggestions today for altering the way in which it works or adding to its functions are unrealistic, unless we can also do something to bridge the gulf, the real political gulf, between individual member countries, about which I shall say more in a moment.

To continue this preliminary train of thought first, however, one of the ideas that has been widely discussed over the years has been altering the level of representation on the Atlantic Council. Today there are permanent ambassadors to the Council from each of the member countries. Every so often ministers come—ministers of finance, foreign ministers, defense ministers—for special meetings. And it has been suggested that there should be someone more on a level with these senior ministers permanently on the Council. But all these ideas have fallen down because in the ordinary way senior ministers cannot be kept in Paris indefinitely without their losing something of their political standing at home, and then the whole idea becomes self-defeating. What I feel, nevertheless, is that, if individual countries want to appoint ministers in order to express their interest and their determination to try to make political co-operation in NATO more effective, they should adopt a practice of doing so, as, in fact, some countries do at the United Nations. I am sure this will not solve the whole problem, but it may help a little.

Then there have been various other suggestions, among them the idea that one way of getting greater cohesion politically would be for the Council to have some kind of intelligence staff of its own for following and interpreting communist moves and propaganda, thus assisting member

nations to react in a more similar way and more quickly.
I don't think myself, that this is a practical proposition. The
right caliber of staff for this kind of specialized operation is
extremely difficult to get, and in any case it is no use having
even the right caliber of staff if politically the countries are
not really ready yet to react in precisely the same way.

Then there have been ideas for improving physical communications. There has been the suggestion recently, which
is an ingenious one, that just as there is a hot line between
Washington and Moscow, so there should now be a hot
line between the individual capitals and the Council Secretariat in Paris. But again this is the cart before the horse.
I think that the communications in a time of crisis are adequate between heads of government; short of that, you are
not going to add very much by making it easier and quicker
for people of the ambassador or junior-minister level to
communicate with one another.

An important and historic suggestion was made by President de Gaulle in 1958 when he demanded a Political
Standing Group, as he called it. This would do on the political side what the Military Standing Group does on the
military side. That is to say, there should be, according to
him, a triumvirate consisting of an American, an English-
man, and a Frenchman who would act as a kind of NATO
cabinet, an internal "ginger group," which would give the
lead in the political affairs of the Atlantic Council. Again,
the objections to this suggestion are many. It was not taken
seriously. The objections are that none of the three, least of
all the United States, of course, would accept any kind of
veto in that sort of organization. If France were in, who
else would want to come in? Of course the Germans would
want to come in. And, if you have the Germans in, who else

might demand the same rights, particularly now that we have the progressive development of the European Economic Community, the Six? In any case, three-power discussions between the Americans, the British, and the French can take place at any time if all three are willing. The notorious fact indeed is that the present crisis, if one likes to call it a crisis, in NATO today, is simply that such discussions are not possible, since the French will not take part in them. To me it is quite evident that the so-called integration of NATO has already gone about as far as it usefully can in present circumstances.

Outside the NATO area, there have been other suggestions concerning closer political co-operation. There is the idea that NATO should have a common policy in dealing with the problems of Southeast Asia, of Viet Nam, of Malaysia, and in the Indian Ocean. There has been a demand for common policies in Africa, that NATO should, in fact, have what has been called a global outlook. But, of course, that is nonsense, too. It is begging the question. It is trying to produce something which would be merely a façade, in that the views of the leading countries on many of these problems, in their interests in them, and the emotions they engender, are inherently different. Furthermore, to have a common policy outside the NATO area would, particularly in Africa, mean having a white front, as it were, against the colored races; and, even if one could achieve it, this would, I think, be inherently undesirable. We would defeat our own ends by creating such a thing.

So I would say that all of these suggestions for closer political co-operation have, in fact, fallen short of the mark and are not any longer the way in which to advance toward a solution to our problems. Before talking about those problems, however, I would just like to say a further word about one or two other things that have happened outside governments, because, after all, political co-operation implies a belief on the part of the member peoples as well as their governments in what is being done and in what should be done. And there have been various non-official efforts in the last few years to create some new machinery, some better means of communication.

Notable among these was the foundation in 1955 of the NATO Parliamentarians—the group of members of the legislatures of each country, roughly two hundred in all, who meet once a year for about a week and who pass resolutions, hear reports, discuss common problems. They have a permanent office in Paris and their meetings have been very useful so far as they go. But these meetings have, of course, no force of law, and they have been limited in effect and in scope. I think, nevertheless, that this is a line which should be developed further. There has been much talk of turning the NATO Parliamentarians into an Atlantic Assembly, into a body which would meet for longer periods of time and which would have certain specific powers, in particular some modest right to review or inspect the financial outlay of the group of NATO nations. Although this would be a major step, I think we ought to try to take it. But, again, this is, of course, only a side issue compared with the main problem of political disagreement among governments.

During 1959, there was an unofficial conference called the NATO Congress in London. I was a member of the International staff of that Congress, and I remember it very well. All these questions of closer integration were discussed. We went round and round them many times, but no special or significant conclusion was reached. Then in January, 1962, there was, I think, a rather valuable meeting. This was an Atlantic Convention, as it was called, which met unofficially in Paris. I was one of the British delegates, and I remember it very well. I recall thrashing out a communiqué, an agreed communiqué, at the end of the convention that became known, among those who took part, as the Declaration of Paris. Today, though the Declaration of Paris is not quite dead, not one single one of its recommendations has ever been carried out by governments; and it is only among those of us who really care about the problem, that what was said is brought again to mind. Yet they were good recommendations, moderately worded, and I would like to summarize them very briefly for you.

We recommended, first of all, that there be a better definition of the principles for which the Western nations stand. This has never been adequately done. It is an extremely difficult task. To say exactly what we do stand for is very hard. We use the words "peace," "democracy," "freedom," "justice"; but the Communists use many of these words, too, and we mean different things by them. Indeed, we Western nations mean different things as between one country and another. We are not even all democratic, and we are not all free, and we are by no means all quite as peaceful as some of our neighbors. To get agreement on this subject is, therefore, peculiarly difficult for the West. But I think it is something which should be attempted, and that it should again be brought to the attention of those who care about the Alliance.

Then we recommended in the Declaration of Paris that there be a Special Commission formed by governments within two years of the convention to study the organization and the more effective implementing of the idea of an Atlantic community. We suggested that in the three usual fields of government—legislative, executive, and judicial—NATO sholud have three appropriate bodies. First of all, as I have already suggested, the NATO Parliamentarians should be turned into an Atlantic Assembly with some sort of formal powers. Secondly, there should be created as an executive what we called a High Council of senior ministers who, meeting from time to time as occasion required, would authorize and establish lines of action for the community as a whole. Thirdly, we recommended on the judicial side that there be a High Court of Justice to settle or give judgment on disputes between members of the NATO alliance themselves. I have often thought since that, if this had come about with the support of the leading governments, it might have made quite some difference in the Greek-Turkish dispute over Cyprus. But, in actuality, not one of these ideas has been implemented; and divisions and divergencies, as I have said, are perhaps greater today than at any time since the treaty was signed.

Now, what are the causes of this change or crisis within NATO? It seems to me that the divisions are so deep that, whatever comes now, it will reflect something essentially different, and therefore new, in the relationships among the member countries. We are, I believe, at this moment in time living through events that may shape our Western World not only up to the end of this first twenty years of the NATO treaty, but well into the 1970's. And I think that three main developments have led to this change.

The primary development has been the mutual acceptance both by the West and by the communist East—that

is, by the Soviet-led part of the communist bloc and by
that part of the Western Alliance which still looks to
Washington for leadership—of a nuclear balance between
the two sides. Since the Cuban Crisis in 1962, neither side
has felt that there can be any meaning to the concept of
victory through nuclear war. There can be war by mistake
perhaps, war by escalation—war as such is still obviously
a danger—but the balance of weapons and the abundance
of "overkill," as it is called, is too great a risk for either
side to accept as a sober calculation. This idea is quite
new in terms of the type of alliance that was signed in
1949.

The next development has been the re-emergence of
Europe. To say this, of course, begs the question of what
we mean by Europe. And a good deal hangs on the view
we take of the political units or lack of unity, the economic
prosperity, and the national attitudes of the various countries that go to make up the modern Europe of the 1960's.
But the basic fact is that in western Europe today many
people no longer feel so dependent on the United States
as they did in the first aftermath of World War II. Whether
they are right or wrong to feel that things have changed
is not the point. The point is that they do feel less dependent, and that this is a new factor. They sense that
the great European civil war, as it has been called, which
began with the turn of the century and flared up into the
two holocausts of World War I and Hitler's war is over.
Although the communist countries of eastern Europe have
not yet recovered, those of western Europe have. And so,
with the development of the nuclear balance, these nations
no longer see the American nuclear umbrella in quite the

same terms as they did before—though I think it accurate to say that the smaller ones have changed their views less and are inherently more content than the larger ones.

This shift in mood is naturally reflected to some degree in the United States. Many Americans see western Europe as thriving and prosperous, able to share more of the economic burden of defense and hence entitled, as well as in duty bound, to share in the ultimate political and military responsibilities as well. All this has had many repercussions. Instead of creating a better sense of purpose, it has promoted a curious loss of confidence. Each of the leading European states is looking for ways of being more independent of the United States, the French deliberately, the Germans because they are disappointed in American reactions to their loyalty, and the British because they are in a difficult position as a result of the disagreements of the other two. The Americans, for their part, while less inclined to give positive leadership to the Alliance, are also less optimistic than they were about the whole concept of Atlantic partnership. Unfortunately, this seems to have become more and more the case in the last two years, since, in fact, President Johnson took over and has allowed himself to be very much preoccupied with domestic affairs. This is a luxury which neither America nor the West can afford.

The third element in this period of revolutionary change through which the West is passing springs from the change in the nature of the cold war itself. Personally, I find it almost as extraordinary that some people still act as if there had been no Russian-Chinese split and no reshaping of the communist threat, as that others seem to go to the opposite extreme and apparently assume that Communists of the Moscow variety will henceforth need only to be treated nicely to be turned into easygoing friends. Neither view, of course, could be further from the truth. The struggle with communism has taken a new turning, and there will undoubtedly be plenty more new turnings before the issue is decided. The mere avoidance of war, however, and the development of coexistence, as we mean the term, can be no more than a kind of armed truce. In reality, the full blossoming of coexistence in the sense that Khrushchev meant it, and all his Soviet successors mean it, represents a state of active political erosion of each side by the other which will continue indefinitely. It is hard for those not directly affected to believe this and hence to understand it; and, from the political point of view, it poses to the Western Alliance internal problems that tend to get worse rather than better.

The key to the solution to the Western dilemma lies in Paris. De Gaulle alone is not the cause of our difficulties, but we certainly cannot resolve them without taking account of what he wants. Then we must either work with him or, if we cannot do that, work knowingly without him. Admittedly, there has recently been some improvement in American-French relations. In December, 1964, President de Gaulle thought fit to speak amiably with the United States Secretary of State, Mr. Dean Rusk. A good deal has been made of the French nuclear force, such as it is, the *force de frappe,* and its being targeted with the allies overall strategic plan as British V-bombers are. But to my mind, all this is superficial. The issues go too deep for tactical displays of this kind to make any basic difference, and it is extremely important to try to understand just what it is that De Gaulle wants, since this is basic to any question of solving the problems of political co-operation at the present time. Is one really right to despair, in fact, of fitting Gaullism into the pattern of Western alliance?

It is widely recognized in Europe that Gaullism is possible only because the Americans are there. If the American presence were not felt in western Europe by virtue of the nuclear shield, of SAC, of the American divisions in Germany, De Gaulle would not be able to think, let alone speak, as he does. But since the United States is there, he has concocted in his own mind a series of concepts in which I personally think he genuinely believes. Muddled and blind to some of the realities of the modern world, these are, nevertheless, the beliefs on which his whole policy is based, and which he will never give up. In some ways what De Gaulle wants is what many Europeans want, including some people in Britain and, indeed, in the British Labor government—but only some. It may be summed up as an independent Europe, a united Europe, and an end to the cold war. The form in which De Gaulle sees these ends, however, and the means by which he would attain them are out of touch with modern history. They are centered on his own person and on the greater glory of France. And I do not believe that in that form they will be accepted by more than a small proportion of the peoples of western Europe. De Gaulle is not only disrupting the Western Alliance, he is also disrupting the movement toward genuine European union. And in doing this, he has, in particular, notoriously confronted the Germans with an agonizing dilemma by trying to make them choose between France and America. This is a choice they should never be called upon to make at this juncture in their history.

In speaking of De Gaulle, I would, nevertheless, like to make one point plain. While I am surprised and alarmed at the amount of wishful thinking that still goes on about Gaullist France, in saying this I speak in sorrow as well as anger. As a young man, I spent many months in France learning the language and the ways of the French, and I came to learn at first hand of so much that they stand for in our Western civilization. I appreciated very fully the quality and the nature of the traditional ties which bound the early years of the American republic with the France of Lafayette. But today, for anyone who has the real interests of the Atlantic Alliance at heart, it is simply no use glossing over the facts.

One of the strangest aspects of our whole problem is that De Gaulle, like others before him, wrote down long ago what he means to do for anyone who cares to read, and yet we either do not bother to read, or we do not believe it when we do. When De Gaulle speaks of independence for Europe, he means a separate policy, a policy of separateness. He does not mean, as some others have meant in recent years when talking about a separate Europe, a kind of twin-pillared Atlantic alliance, with the United States on one side and a kind of United States of Europe on the other. He means a Europe which would go its own way, not necessarily hostile to the United States, but separate. It may have quite friendly relations with America, but this would be incidental. It will not be a Third Force in quite the sense that this term was originally used—that is, a floating element aloof from and somewhere between the two opposite poles of the United States and the Soviet Union. Rather will it be by definition a regrouping of all the European peoples themselves, playing a separate role under the umbrella of French nuclear force. It will be, and this De Gaulle has said with perfect seriousness several times, a new Europe stretching from the Channel to the Urals.

Western Europe, that is, is not a political entity in its own right; it is part of Europe as a whole, including the present communist states of eastern Europe and including the European areas of Russia itself.

De Gaulle, of course, is not consistent. Much of what he says is self-contradictory, as when he talks about the nature of the Europe which he seeks to create. It will be, he declares, a Europe *des patries,* a Europe of nation states. Although claiming to speak for a united and independent Europe, that is, De Gaulle rejects automatically the very kind of progress toward supranationality which has been so carefully and painstakingly made during the past few years in such organisms as the European Economic Community, the Coal and Steel Pool, and even the Organization for Economic Co-operation and Development. International integration must take its time; more harm than good will come of trying to rush it. And in this, perhaps, De Gaulle is right. The conditions of modern Europe, for instance, are not those of the early years of the American republic. But unless the direction taken is the right one, even if progress toward it is slow, we shall never reach the right end. The Gaullist concept of Europe is pointed in the wrong direction, it is a contradiction in itself, and it is out of tune with the twentieth century.

De Gaulle is also in a way inconsistent when he talks about communism. The truth is that he does not take the communists seriously. Although he is building up a nuclear military force of his own, he does not really believe that the communist enemy exists. He sees the Soviet Union more as a nation state than as the driving force of a revolutionary ideology. He disputes, to my mind, the whole premise on which the North Atlantic Treaty is based. And, since he thinks that, it is small wonder to me that he is unwilling to pay what he regards as the political price needed to keep the Alliance going—namely, acceptance of American leadership, retention of nuclear responsibility in American hands, and the presence of American forces under NATO in western Europe.

In some ways De Gaulle's own political success inside France has misled him. The large Communist Party and the even larger communist vote in France failed to prevent him from obtaining and then keeping power. But the reasons for this were, of course, the special ones of recent French history and French national emotion. De Gaulle stands for something unique in French eyes that perhaps even he has not properly understood. And to mix this very special situation with his own concepts of national states and of a dimension to international affairs not seriously different from that of fifty years ago is to close the mind, I think, to most of the lessons of the present era. It is to live, in a sense, in the age of steam when one is really in the age of jet propulsion.

Then on Germany, which is the heart in many ways both of the problems of political co-operation within the Alliance and of dealing with the Soviet Union, De Gaulle is again contradictory. He calls for unity in Europe, speaking of east and west Europe. And with Chancellor Adenauer he signed a treaty of friendship between France and Germany, which I think can reasonably be claimed to set the seal on the end of that great European civil war to which I referred. But Europe as a whole still remains divided between east and west, and, while De Gaulle has it in mind to make a bid for some new understanding with Russia, it is his fundamental aim to keep Germany divided. I think the old fears in that respect are still there. Although he is sincere enough in dedicating himself to the building of a new relationship with the Federal German Republic that we know in Bonn, it is no part of his plan to see a fully reunited Germany step into the shoes of this smaller democratic Germany of the West. If it came to German reunification, De Gaulle would almost certainly seek to make a deal with Russia that would carry with it some form of German neutralization and, if that happened, there would be nothing left whatever of our present Atlantic Alliance and of NATO. In reality, of course, German reunion is still not a matter of practical politics because the Russians will not risk it. But that will assuredly not stop De Gaulle from playing with it in his own mind and on his own terms.

I feel, therefore, as you can see, that De Gaulle has reached a point where he is acting, and has been acting for perhaps two years at least, against the best interests of France and against the best interests of the Alliance. He has done this by challenging his allies and by raising issues of political co-operation which have already gone a long way toward making NATO unworkable. Where, then, do we stand now? There have been discussions, as you know, and a great deal of comment in the press and from politicians about the problem of nuclear control. There has been a suggestion of a multilateral force, the MLF, and now of the ANF, the Atlantic Nuclear Force, since it is in terms of nuclear control that these problems of political co-operation have recently become most practical and most urgent. And it is, of course, on this very question that the refusal of the French to have any part in any new scheme is most pointed, thus damaging the machinery of the Alliance in other respects as well.

This problem of nuclear control is relevant both to the big deterrent itself, the ultimate strategic use of the supreme weapon, and to the kind of tactical confrontation which might develop, in the first instance at any rate, on the flanks of NATO, in northern Norway, or in Turkey if there were a threat to the Straits. In dealing with these problems of control, one of the points that I, as a European, feel most strongly is that the ultimate word must lie with the President of the United States. It must, for one thing, lie with one man; it cannot be held by a committee, and there is obviously no other man in the Western World who is in a position to exercise that kind of control. Therefore, in a sense, what the rest of us must do is to have more say in the vital discussions of the factors involved when the American President is making up his mind. But that is only one aspect of it. The other aspect is how, in fact, one can give individual members of the Alliance, other than the United States and to some extent Britain, a better understanding of the facts of the nuclear problem by enabling them to gain their own experience from actually handling nuclear weapons. And it is in this respect that the suggestions for a special multilateral nuclear force are particularly important.

The reasons for suggesting such a force are obviously more political than military, though I am not personally one of the many who rule out the idea that the force would have any military relevance at all. And because it is a political more than a military issue, the solution to this nuclear problem is something which is going to preoccupy the countries of the Alliance throughout 1965, if not into 1966 and even beyond. Of the attitudes of the leading members of the Alliance I would say the following. The United States was originally, perhaps, over-anxious that something should be done, but has now gone too far the other way in washing its hands of the problem. The MLF was promoted very largely by President Kennedy. It was taken up after his death by President Johnson. Now that it has been dropped, there is a curious aloofness on the American side. This seems to be the case in spite of the fact that the United States is just as committed in practice to the defense of western Europe as it ever was, and that Americans feel this more surely perhaps than at any previous time in the Alliance. But it does mean, as I suggested, that the biggest member of the Alliance is receding emotionally both in terms of its government action and in terms perhaps of popular opinion from the idea of Atlantic partnership; and that, I think, is a pity. I feel that something will need to change in this respect if we are going to get over the problem of the split in the Alliance which France has created.

In Germany, as I have already suggested, there is suddenly and curiously a disillusionment with America. This is partly due to the approach of a German general election in September, 1965. Successive German governments have failed to get any further with the idea of reuniting Germany, and so there is some reaction against depending on America to help achieve this. There has also been a realization in Germany that President Johnson, at any rate, is not prepared at present to have the kind of special relationship with Western Germany to which a number of Germans have aspired. A good many people in Germany too, like those in France and Britain and other west European countries, feel some pull from the idea that, since Europe itself has recovered, Europeans ought to get together to resolve their own problems without an American hand on their shoulders.

In Britain, at this period of political disarray within the Alliance, there is not yet any great leaning toward Europe on the part of the Labor government, though the Conservatives, in opposition, have recently restated the case for joining the Six of the Common Market. The government's two main interests are in making new efforts to reach some further agreement with the Soviet Union, and in fostering, rather surprisingly, the attachment to the United States. It seems to me that the British Prime Minister, Mr. Harold Wilson, and President Johnson have got on well together when they have met, and, since both are good politicians, this seems to provide ground for hoping that, as the months go by, their two countries will understand each other better.

The smaller countries of the Alliance are, as I have suggested, much more content with things as they are, with the existing degree of political co-operation—or lack of it—and with the American nuclear umbrella. On the other hand, they, too, have been roused by this idea of a pan-Europe, which was to some extent inherent in the proposals for a multilateral force. Therefore, they are not uninterested in the kind of things that De Gaulle is saying. But, of course, when one says the smaller nations, there are certain notable exceptions. The most notable is undoubtedly Canada which, by definition, is naturally not concerned in the pan-European idea and has a special position in relation to the United States. To some extent, Norway and Denmark are also exceptions, since they want nothing to do with nuclear weapons—for obvious reasons. They are close to Russia; they are small; there is the sentiment of their people, which is very understandable, in this respect. And so, in a sense, they are more willing to carry on if possible with the existing structure and the present limping degree of political co-operation.

None of these smaller countries wants a French hegemony instead of an American one. None would accept that there is any real substitute for the American nuclear umbrella, and certainly not this tiny, probably altogether ineffective French nuclear force that is being so laboriously built up. It seems, nevertheless, that the position and mood are such that we must have some new form of organizational control over nuclear forces. I do not think this can come before the German general elections, nor probably until the French presidential election is out of the way—until, that is, we know rather than suspect that De Gaulle, if his health is good enough, will both stand and be re-elected again. If and when the members of NATO can ultimately resume active and positive discussion of a new international nuclear structure, however, it is essential not only that the final veto remain in American hands, but also, that the United States agree to surrender some real element of control in the planning stage.

This means leaving De Gaulle out of it, while at the same time leaving room for France to come in after De Gaulle has gone. But it also means recognizing the validity of the greater-Europe ideas which De Gaulle speaks about. To achieve any worthwhile result in this extremely complicated and frustrating situation, I feel that more positive support for some of the present British efforts to negotiate with the Germans is required from the American side, since without it the pull of France seems bound to be too strong. It is, therefore, at least a step in the right direction that President Johnson has recently made it rather clearer to the

Germans that, although he does not wish at present to take a more constructive part in the negotiations over the British proposal for an Atlantic Nuclear Force (ANF) he believes that the American presence is just as essential to the future of western Europe and of Germany as it has been in the past.

Throughout this survey of the dilemmas into which the Atlantic Alliance is now plunged, I have attempted to show two things. One is that political co-operation in NATO is at the lowest ebb it has so far reached. But the other is that the need for the Alliance and hence the call for political co-operation is as strong as ever it was. All this means that, if there is any one lesson which we should learn from the past, it is that no political structure will stand the weight of history unless its foundations are laid in the concrete of up-to-date realities. I believe that the form of the 1949 NATO treaty is now out of date. But I also believe that we can and should revise it to meet the needs of today.

One of these needs, the one that is paramount, is that in any revision of NATO we must recognize the new position of western Europe in relation to the United States. As I have implied several times, President de Gaulle is being as successful as he is in his deliberate disruption of the Alliance because he is appealing to a widespread European emotion. He is, nevertheless, prostituting it to his own ends, and the task of those who believe in the future of the Atlantic community is to harness this new European maturity to the right purpose. For this the most practical preliminary need is an acceptable solution to the problem of nuclear control. Moreover, this has to be achieved without provoking a violent reaction on the other side of the Iron Curtain, since our aim must be to bring about a further lowering of East-

West tension. Through the type of firm yet flexible negotiation with the Russians now favored in most of the Atlantic capitals, and not least in Washington, this new NATO which we are seeking must somehow move forward toward a system of arms control, and so to a more permanent basis for peace than the present tacit, but brittle, balance of nuclear power. Only then can we solve the ever nagging and constantly dangerous problem of Germany.

For all these reasons, I believe that the greatest importance still attaches to the proposals for an Atlantic Nuclear Force, and in particular to the emergence of the virtual inevitability of taking its center of political control out of any existing NATO organization. I await with the very greatest interest the development of this idea, since it cannot fail to have a dramatic effect on the position and influence of the present Atlantic Council. Naturally, I hope that this effect will bring about a higher real degree of political cooperation in NATO, even if the form is somewhat different. For of one thing I am certain: if we are going to keep the Western Alliance alive during these next few difficult years, we cannot afford to sacrifice the substance for the shadow. And unless we can all recognize this and work for it, we shall none of us achieve the kind of freedom, the kind of self-respect, and the kind of international security which alone is meaningful in the nuclear age.

Paul Stehlin

Some French Reflections on the Alliance

IN 1969, NATO will have had twenty years of existence, and
the question of its survival will have to be answered. In
pondering the future of our Alliance, its form and its substance, as well as in attempting to understand the present
state of affairs within NATO, it is advisable to look back to
the past, to the circumstances under which the North
Atlantic Treaty was adopted.

When the treaty was signed in 1949, the intention of the
Soviet Union to pursue her advance toward the west was
obvious. Already she had set up in a number of eastern
European countries forms of government of her own choice,
and her last move, in Czechoslovakia, put the Russian

advanced position at less than a hundred miles from the
Rhine—and the French border!

The first demonstration of Western solidarity in the face
of threats from the Soviet Union had been the signing of the
Treaty of Dunkirk in 1947 between France and Great
Britain. It was followed, a year later, by the Treaty of
Brussels, concluded among France, Great Britain, Belgium,
Holland, and Luxembourg. It is worthwhile to reflect a
moment upon the latter treaty, for it gave birth to what
later became known as the Western Union. The intention of
those responsible for the treaty was to create an alliance of
a new type. They were seeking a concentration of effort—
economic and industrial, with a prospective pooling of
resources—which would allow them to increase their out-
put of armaments and to raise their technical capabilities to
a level comparable to the latest American achievements,
and at no greater total cost. This was, of course, considered
a long-term aim.

Although President Truman declared to Congress: "I
am certain that the determination of the European free
countries to protect themselves will be followed by the
same determination on our part to help them in doing so,"
European statesmen demonstrated in the way they negotiated the North Atlantic Treaty that they feared they
had gone too far in the direction of European union. They
preferred direct protection by the United States to reliance
on a European organization which could have raised itself, with American assistance, to the level of true partnership with equal responsibilities, duties, rights, and efforts.
The first opportunities offered by the Treaty of Brussels
were, therefore, lost—the possibility of arranging British

participation in a European organization; the possibility of initiating on a realistic basis a program for uniting Europe; and the possibility of achieving recognition by the European countries concerned of the place defense should have in national policy.

Since his return to leadership, General de Gaulle has often emphasized the need for all European nations to contribute to their own national defense. To rely on an ally for protection results in a nation's becoming disinterested in national security and in its accompanying failure to allocate a sufficient part of its total national budget for military expenditures.

The establishment of effective national defense systems in Europe involves problems not confronted by the United States, which can afford a budget covering all the requirements for her total security. Broadly speaking, the defense budget of each European country varies with its relative national income. But all have one thing very much in common: all are substantially below the level required to maintain an independent national defense policy. This is clearly evident and widely recognized.

The European countries are, therefore, confronted with two choices. The first is to maintain the status quo, to continue primarily to depend on the unilateral protection of the United States while maintaining and developing forces supplementing those of their ally. These forces are largely conventional; the limited nuclear contributions are weapons on loan from the United States which remain under ultimate American control. The other choice is more dignified and more worthy of Europe's history and culture. It is for the European countries to unite for their common defense, to create through economic and industrial concentration the conditions comparable to those in the United States which are required for over-all security.

It appears today that there is no way within the Alliance to reconcile the divergent attitudes reflected in these two choices. The fear of losing the benefit of immediate and powerful American protection induces most political leaders in Europe to declare that they are satisfied with the present state of the Alliance and to accept unilateral dependence on, and leadership of, the United States. Actually, the imminent danger against which NATO was created has been averted, and the number and intensity of threats which reappear now and then for a short time are decreasing continuously. These threats do, however, help keep NATO together, though they have no effect on possible changes in the form of the Alliance.

Thus we remain within an organization that is politically and militarily characterized by a lack of balance between the United States and her divided allies. But there is more to be said. If we consider each of the countries separately, we observe that their national viewpoints concerning the development of their forces have prevailed over their intention to participate in a harmonized construction for common defense.

The examples of Great Britain, France and Germany, in particular, point up this fact. Through twenty-four years of close association, Great Britain has become accustomed to benefiting from the assistance of the United States, and has consequently secured modern means of defense, including, notably, a strategic nuclear power. Under the aura of equality, however, she actually submits to a status of dependence on American military strength, judging, no doubt, that it is mandatory for her security. It is likely that the present British Labor government will strengthen that position. Britain's national effort will probably be more intimately associated with the forces of NATO, which in practice means expanding her military co-operation, mainly in the nuclear field, with the United States.

France, for her part, estimates that a sound defense policy is not compatible with an integration of her forces within the Alliance. Since 1958, she has been making the effort to provide herself with modern military equipment and armaments, both conventional and nuclear, to the extent permitted by her budgetary resources. She has also requested, making it a condition of her continued participation in NATO, a responsibility equal to that of the United States and Great Britain in the conduct of the over-all strategy of common defense. In addition, and in line with the principle of a classical coalition, she wishes to be free to employ her forces for any action she judges necessary, either jointly with other countries or on her own.

Germany, the last of the three, differs fundamentally from Great Britain in that all her forces are subordinated to an integrated allied command and her defense budget is exclusively assigned to conventional armament.

Thus Great Britain and France, on the one hand, are both anxious—though with different motivations—to acquire all the armaments which modern techniques can produce; Germany, on the other, must concentrate her efforts on conventional armaments. The result is growing divergencies and a lack of balance and harmony within the Alliance. The quantitative and qualitative superiority in military organization and equipment of the United States continues to grow because her three leading European partners can afford no larger contribution. And so we are confronted with disparate attitudes on the part of the European countries toward the United States, disparate ideas as to the degree of dependence they are willing to accept—and an absence of a unified NATO defense Doctrine.

The most serious conflict between Europe and America is over nuclear strategy, and it endangers the future of NATO beyond 1969. To achieve a solution, logic requires that the United States encourage European countries in the Alliance to set aside their differences and agree among themselves upon a European defense doctrine. The United States would continue her present commitment to NATO, but would, in addition, stand ready to help her allies if they developed a realistic plan for a European nuclear deterrent.

In the process of making decisions regarding their own defense, the Europeans should be aware that the nuclear age has not invalidated the principle that a threat can only be checked by forces which are comparable, equal, or superior in quality and quantity to those of the enemy. No other valid explanation can be offered for the continuing race between the United States and the Soviet Union to produce more and more powerful weapons in abundant and overabundant quantity. Intellectual speculations on how an opponent would react when faced with a country, or group of countries, with a military strength notably inferior to his own, especially in nuclear armaments, are often attempts to prove that what is economically, financially, and industrially feasible is also militarily sufficient. Such artificial arguments should have no place in planning a defense policy.

It is without doubt the "nuclear factor" which under-
mines the guarantees the Alliance can offer. The doctrine
which was valid in the mid-1950's is today out of place.
The existence of the nuclear arsenals of the United States
and the Soviet Union means—and it is a truism to say so—
that the risks the American nation might possibly have to
take now to defend her allies have increased to such an
extent since the Treaty of 1949 that her allies must re-
appraise the value of the guarantees of their national
security that it provides in the light of present conditions.
The risk of massive destruction of American territory in
the event of a United States nuclear intervention in favor
of a European ally is incomparably greater than it was
fifteen years ago. It is, therefore, proper and realistic to
reflect upon the considerable diminution of the guarantees
which the Treaty could offer in 1949 (and during the
whole period of the American monopoly and supremacy),
and to start negotiations toward an arrangement which
would provide equal and firm guarantees to all members
of the Alliance. In the prevailing state of affairs in NATO,
and for the reasons I have indicated, the French government believes it is essential to a country threatened with
destruction to possess her own national nuclear force and
to exercise direct control over the means of nuclear action.
This raises the question, from an operational point of view,
of the practical value of the French deterrent capability.
Our effort in nuclear armaments is subject to a wide variety of interpretations, both within and outside NATO.
One opinion is that the American guarantee is valid to
the fullest extent in any event; but to this the French would
answer that since under certain circumstances a nation
could be tempted to act out of self-interest, it is essential

to be master of one's own security. To this response comes
immediately the objection that the French nuclear effort is
useless anyway. The French reply is that in the nuclear
age, when we confront a nuclear threat, the question is not
one of ratio of forces but of acceptable or unacceptable
risk. Such widely divergent opinions show that a nuclear
strategy still belongs, fortunately, to the realm of theory.

From my point of view—and I speak as one who is as
confident in the association with the United States as he is
convinced of the necessity of western Europe's modifying
the form and the nature of her contribution to the Alliance
—the problem is one of assuming equal responsibility and
developing a capacity to oppose and face a nuclear threat.
Though it is likely that no solution can warrant absolute
security, a concerted action by the European nations of
NATO to provide themselves with operable nuclear armament would reinforce the American guarantee.

The Multilateral Nuclear Force was, in my opinion, a
serious and sincere attempt by the United States government to share with European countries the responsibility
for controlling the use of nuclear weapons and participating in the provision and maintenance of them. One may,
however, first question the practicality of the military
structure proposed. The choice of ships equipped with
Polaris missiles and manned by interallied crews can
hardly escape criticism from a purely technical and professional standpoint. Moreover, human integration carried
to such a degree affects efficiency. Second, the strategic
action of such a force would be essentially counter-city;
and in this area, the American means are overabundant
and have a capacity of destruction many times superior
to the potential necessary to annihilate the Soviet Union.

Third, the employment of the MLF remains subordinated to the exercise by the President of the United States of the right reserved to him alone to decide for or against the use of nuclear weapons. This requirement of American consent results in the present state of unilateral dependence upon American assistance. One might say that the European countries, too, could stop the MLF from acting; but one can in no way compare these as reciprocal possibilities since the MLF would be very small indeed compared with the independent American nuclear capability. That is why I have come to the conclusion that the MLF would not help the European countries of NATO to reconcile and harmonize their views on a common defense concept. It does not reassure the Europeans that the United States will really risk nuclear war to defend Europe. If we consider the position adopted by the various countries in NATO, there remains only Germany for which the MLF would be, politically, a substitute for an independent nuclear deterrent.

The French national effort to attain a strategic nuclear force has been criticized many times as a factor causing dissension and division within NATO. I believe that the MLF proposal should at least have been made a basis for discussion; however, since it has been examined bilaterally, the project has so far served only to separate further those European nations which consider it essential that they retain complete responsibility for the elaboration and management of their defense, from those others that are satisfied with the guaranteed protection of a powerful ally on whom they unilaterally depend.

It is most surprising to observe the obstinacy of certain politicians in guarding the national economic interests of their countries while indicating at the same time that they are ready to leave national defense to the judgment and care of an ally. The basic reason for the lack of importance assigned to national defense in Europe, as contrasted with the United States, is the spread between levels of information and knowledge, a spread which is to the prejudice of Europe. When compared to the magnitude of the great American unity, our capabilities—scientific, technical, and industrial—shrink to the size of our individual countries.

Although some progress has been made toward economic unity, in defense we remain divided, as I have shown in the cases of the three major European countries in NATO. It is in the definite interest of the United States to help to remedy our division by encouraging us to put forward our own European proposal for unity, rather than trying to impose a ready-made American solution such as the MLF. To follow this course the United States would have to abandon wishing to remain in exclusive charge of the use of nuclear arms. The present American attitude of opposing a proliferation of nuclear weapons, however understandable it is for the sake of peace and survival, does not take into account the legitimate will of an allied nation to exert a direct control over the nuclear arms it considers indispensable for its security. The strategy which was valid as long as there was an American nuclear monopoly, supremacy, or evident superiority, was invalidated for a European country from the moment the Soviet Union acquired a comparable nuclear power. It then became essential for the European members of the Alliance to seek ways to change the essence of their contribution to the common security. If the country cannot, through its own capacity, make this contribution, nor itself present a sizable deterrent capability, the logical aim is to seek an association of countries united by the natural links of geography which would allow a pooling of resources to meet the need for nuclear defense and defense in general.

A good way, in my opinion, for the United States to acknowledge the advisability of such an association would be to regard favorably the establishment of an entente of European countries and to switch from the formula of a multilateral force to direct and provisional procurement of nuclear weapons for a European defense organization. The first task of the organization would be to create a nuclear strategic force in line with an agreement of common defense in the spirit of the Brussels Treaty of 1948. The next step would be for Europe, by its own means, to set up a strategic nuclear force of sufficient strength to meet the estimated threat to Europe and to parallel this with convergent economic and industrial efforts leading to political association and unity.

It is often said that proposals of this kind would be opposed on two counts. It is asserted that the American government fears the spread of nuclear arms authority over Western defense. Critics also argue the levels of logic in establishing a European nuclear power before a controlling political authority has been created. It is true that at the recent meeting between General de Gaulle and Chancellor Erhard much emphasis was placed on political unity within Europe and that consideration of a common European defense took second place. It remains to be seen, however, how the points of agreement reached during their talk will be realized in practice.

The present state of stagnation in Europe in regard to common defense and political unity results from the struggle between those who want to do something, however modest the first steps may appear to be, and those who reject every partial solution in favor of immediate and total unity.

The extensive experience I have had since 1945 with efforts toward European unity leads me to conclude that one achievement produces another. There has been too much emphasis on integration of forces. The problems with which we are confronted are essentially economic and industrial. To solve the economic problem we must establish conditions which enable us, like the United States, to provide means necessary and sufficient to provide for our defense. To solve the industrial problem, we must create the capacity required for the production of modern armaments.

From a political and organizational point of view, this plan would lead to a bipolar structure of the Alliance; that is, to a United Europe on one side and the United States on the other, but with both operating in close cooperation. The aim is, if I may put it a different way, to make western Europe a defense unity capable by itself of executing all commitments for its own security. The Alliance would not be, as it is today, a complementary association for defense in which Europe is unilaterally dependent upon the United States, but a partnership in which each partner would independently be responsible for its own defense affairs, while enjoying the supplementary guarantee of mutual assistance, with equal rights, duties, and national capabilities.

Such a European defense unity should be carried forward in stages, in a pragmatic manner, with the purpose of achieving a military power corresponding to the nature of the threat and in proportion to its size. The establishment of a balance of strength and responsibility within the Alliance would contribute to the elimination of the tensions and divergencies which impede and sometimes paralyze its proper functioning.

Since, as I have already said, one of the greatest difficulties in the Alliance results from the differences in points of view regarding the nature of the relations which should be established between the United States and the European countries—specifically, in the degree of dependence Europe should have on the United States—the American government should encourage every effort toward European unity. What Europe needs is not American aid as it was given in the past, however indispensable it was when NATO was first established, but American cooperation in bringing to a united Europe a defense capability as equal as possible to that of the United States. This would involve two factors: (1) technological assistance which would relieve the European allies from expenditures of time, resources, and energy to discover what has already been invented and even produced; and (2) assistance in developing a modern defense concept in Europe.

Though it is wrong to generalize, the fact remains that often people in Europe who bear the responsibility for national security do not have a realistic doctrine of defense. They look upon military forces as an end in themselves, rather than as instruments of total defense which in volume and composition must bear a direct relation to the size and nature of the estimated threat. The philosophical concept of deterrence, which for lack of a better word we call "dissuasion," is often talked about but not always with a proper understanding of its meaning. It is not enough to note that deterrence cannot be measured, nor to observe that for the United States and the Soviet Union it means possession of the largest possible number of nuclear weapons. And it is wrong to reason that what is economically feasible in France, whose budget limits production capabilities to a small percentage of what the United States can afford, is thereby sufficient. Greater knowledge of American defense practices and policies will direct the countries of Europe to a realistic concept of their own defense.

Hopefully, a united Europe, once it is established as an equal partner with the United States within the Alliance, would represent a step toward an Atlantic Community institutionally formulated to meet the political requirements of defense and prosperity. In this Community, political thinking will have to follow the upward march to which science and technology are inviting it.

When he takes the trouble to think about the significance of the more and more powerful and far-reaching modern weapons and their capacity for instantaneous destruction, the military man—so often blamed in the past for preparing for war—is alarmed to see politics still confined within the rules of a game that is no longer of our age. Though the political mind is bound to lag behind the pace set by scientific and technological progress (it always has), the sudden and revolutionary growth in the power of weapons and the range of their carriers that has occurred since 1945 demand an overhaul of present political divisions in Europe. A new structure must be devised, one which will have the capacity to create and control the forces produced by the discoveries of our time. I have tried to demonstrate why that structure will have to precede a larger community; the progression will be, in brief: a united Europe, an Atlantic partnership, and an Atlantic world.

The first step, a united Europe, should not and would not be continent-oriented in its approach to economic and foreign affairs. Though the initiative and procedure for establishing such a union should be left to the European countries themselves, the United States should encourage them in developing their own defense organization and power. Mr. George Ball, Undersecretary of State, did just this in a speech of May 8, 1964: "If Europe were sufficiently far advanced toward political unity that it could manage and control an atomic deterrent, we could look forward to an effective and integrated Atlantic defense founded on a true nuclear partnership."

It has been said—in the United States, of course, but also in Europe and especially in Great Britain—that a united Europe, once it had acquired the means to a new great power, would pursue an independent strategy. This argument has resulted in two conflicting conclusions. One group contends that an independent European strategy would defeat projects such as MLF, which seek to prevent the emergence of independent nuclear forces. Another group holds that European assumption of the full burden for its own defense would release the United States from its "untangling" alliance. I do not believe that views of this sort play a role in the thoughts of policy-makers, be they American or European, who give serious and expert consideration to the harmonious and efficient organization of the Western World that are essential to its defense and survival.

I remember that when I studied philosophy in school, one of the first rules of morals we were taught was "Act as if your behavior could become universal law." This precept can be expanded beyond the individual; it is also valid for human communities—for Europe and the western Atlantic world. It means, to my mind, that an organization, even one limited to defense, must be founded on the fundamental human principles of freedom and equality if it is to achieve its purpose. A European structure has to proceed from a European choice (though this does not exclude outside advice and assistance) in order for Europe to become a great power able to care for its own security.

Security is, however, in the last analysis, dependent on the economic and industrial capabilities of the new power and, in addition, on the magnitude of the threat to which it is exposed. Any objective consideration of the present state of the world and its foreseeable future must lead to the conclusion that the structure of Europe, as it evolves on the basis of its own free choice, has to be undertaken in conjunction with preparation for an Atlantic partnership.

It is true that Europe needs the United States more than the other way round, and that even a united Europe could not do without American support and guarantees in a confrontation with the Soviet Union. But it is wishful thinking to assume that the two elements of the Atlantic Alliance are and will be confronted by the Soviet Union alone; for more and more we shall be confronted by two major communist powers. The rivalry between them does not play in our favor; on the contrary, their competition, which is not merely ideological in character, may well hasten the spread of communism to parts of the world essential to Western security. I have in mind especially Africa, geographically so close to western Europe and the first and most important objective of Soviet indirect strategy before the United States became the final objective of the communist world revolution. That is why I believe it is loose talk and a waste of time to try to evaluate who needs whom the most within the Free World.

The United States of America is enjoying the greatest security possible in the present world because it is a powerful federation of states. It offers an example of what western European countries must do to survive. With the establishment of a comparable European union, it will be possible for the two to enter into a true partnership which can create the new dimensions necessary to protect the Free World against the dynamic foreign policies to which the Soviet Union and Communist China are committed in order to maintain their governments. These two are doomed to act together.

The concept of a united Europe lies halfway between two alternate extremes: on the one hand, a unilateral American guarantee to Europe, which entails American leadership in the defense strategy of the West and the right of veto over the use of nuclear weapons; and, on the other hand, a conclusion that the Alliance is outmoded and useless. The first, as we have seen, divides the Alliance; the second would mean the end of collective security and a reversion to international chaos.

In the early years of the Alliance, the unilateral dependence of western Europe on American nuclear power was satisfactory and necessary, but present circumstances have altered this situation. The indirect strategy now being applied by the Soviet Union and Communist China requires that the United States base its long-term security more and more on the contributions which the European countries of NATO can make in neutralizing and, if need be, opposing

Russian and Chinese attempts to resume their territorial advance, either in Europe or in areas nearby.

In the light of this background, I conclude that if NATO is to survive after 1969, the three progressive stages toward an Atlantic world which I have outlined should be adopted as the general policy of the Atlantic Council. There is, however, no reason to take a pessimistic view of the future. The verbal exchanges between governments and the decisions they will have to reach must reflect the wisdom of the peoples and their natural instinct for self-preservation, and this means an ever stronger American-European solidarity.

Horst Blomeyer

Germany in NATO

TO DISCUSS THE SITUATION of the Federal Republic inside
the North Atlantic Treaty Organization means to discuss
almost all the problems of the alliance—because they all
affect Germany to a very high degree and in all of them
the Federal Republic has to take and to defend a position.
I shall limit myself to only a few questions, but—it seems
to me—they are the basic ones.

The problems which the Atlantic Alliance has now to
face originate, as I see it, mainly from the technological developments of the last fifteen years. The emergence of the
Soviet Union as a nuclear superpower, the invention of
nuclear-tipped intercontinental rockets in the Soviet Union
as well as in the United States, have thoroughly affected the
politico-military equation on which NATO was originally

based. The so-called nuclear stalemate has cast doubt on
the credibility of the U.S. deterrent in the case of a Soviet
threat in Central Europe. The dangerous consequences of
this change are, however, somewhat compensated by the
feeling which seems to exist in East and West alike that
any "hot war" between the two big nuclear powers could
possibly lead to escalation into a general nuclear war. The
result is that *because of the existing engagement of the
United States in Europe,* a relatively stable situation exists
on the European Continent, and concurrently a feeling pre-
vails that there is no imminent threat to be feared from
the Soviet Union. This feeling has negative effects on the
cohesion of the alliance. Usually, in peacetime an organization for the common defense of a group of nations will
only be persuasive as long as a real and credible threat
exists—and, of course, only as long as it suits the varying
interests of the different partners.

The present discussion inside NATO on strategy, on force
goals, on participation in the nuclear field emerges from
basic changes in the environment, to which the alliance
must adjust. It is only natural that there are different opinions among the parties to the Alliance: the elements from
which the military-political considerations must start are
different from country to country. What we have to try to
find is a common denominator for our diverging attitudes
concerning necessity, scope, and organization of a Western
defense.

It is in my country's interest to make her specific problems as clear as possible—because we believe that Germany's geographical and political situation plays a key role
in these considerations. Probably, no other country is more
aware of the necessity of the Alliance than the Federal

Republic of Germany. Germany happens to be in the area of the most significant military confrontation between the Soviet bloc and the Western Alliance. Not only is she situated in the center of Europe, but also she has an economic potential that makes her a prime target for Soviet expansionism. Twenty Soviet divisions concentrated in the Soviet-occupied zone of Germany present so large a threat that the Federal Republic must look around for support and guarantees for her security. To be included in the balance of deterrence as part of the Western system is for Germany a matter of life and death. Only if her link with the Alliance and, thereby, with the pre-eminent Western power, the United States, is such that the political adversary cannot hope to isolate her, can she expect to participate in the blessings of the Western deterrent and, consequently, of the nuclear stalemate.

This is one of the reasons for Germany's interest in military integration inside the armed forces of the Atlantic world, in the conventional as well as in the nuclear fields. The more tightly knit the Alliance is and the less chance of miscalculation by an enemy, the greater is the chance of every single member's sharing the deterrent benefits of American nuclear power. The presence of a substantial body of American troops on German territory is for the German people, as well as for the Soviet Union, the most evident and convincing proof of irrevocable U.S. commitment.

It is the exposed geographical position of the Federal Republic of Germany which presents us more than in the case of any other country with one of the most critical questions in the Alliance: Is it reasonable and can we, for all practical purposes, afford to rely entirely on the effect of the great American deterrence? Is it true that the possibility of any conflict's escalating into general nuclear war indeed prevents the enemy from *all kinds* of hostile actions? Is it not likely that the enemy would be tempted to run the risk of hostilities on a lower level, expecting that the West would decide to avoid a nuclear exchange? Can it be excluded from possibility that the enemy might doubt that the U.S. would resort to nuclear weapons for the defense of Europe—action which would lead to the destruction of the very region which it aimed to defend, Central and western Europe? There is a possibility of countless misunderstandings and miscalculations. Preparedness for immediate reaction on all levels and to all kinds of aggression is for Germany indispensable. We have no space which would give us and our allies time to consider when to counterattack. Our territory is tremendously narrow, only 125 miles in some parts. We cannot risk the loss of territory —a reconquest would be a matter of years probably—and, even then, what would we find to liberate?

Therefore, our basic philosophy is by nature opposite to that once called the philosophy of sea powers: Since land attack on a sea power was not possible, that power was assured of enough time to build an invasion army. The Continental power, on the other hand, surrounded by neighbors, must be ready for an early attack—and the more diversified, quick, and effective its system of mobilization, the better its chance to win a war. The Continental concept of an awareness of imminent threat has long been part of German military thinking.

This difference in concepts has its parallel in the nuclear field. The more distant nations are from the line of direct contact with the enemy, the more they believe in relying on general deterrence. This is only natural: an attack on the United States, or on Great Britain, with conventional weapons is practically impossible; if, against all likelihood, it did happen, it would be evident that a fight for life and death was being sought by the enemy. The question of minor hostilities and how to react to them does not confront the United States and Great Britain proper. With some variations, the same is true for an attack on France. All three nations cannot hope to have time to build up their defense systems in case of war—they are also tempted to rely on their nuclear deterrent and disregard conventional armament; they, as well as the enemy, know that a decisive fight among nuclear powers would finally lead to employment of nuclear weapons and to general nuclear war, a prospect which is unacceptable to both sides. In the German case, to find out whether an armed hostility is minor or serious can be definitely established only by time—time which we would not have. A pronounced policy on the part of the West to first examine size and scope of hostile action before making a response would serve as an invitation to the opponent to risk at least minor ventures—an inducement to miscalculation on the side of the enemy. A forward strategy, however, with a declared preparedness to use battlefield nuclear weapons, if necessary, might deter the enemy from all, even "minor," intrusions. Such readiness does not, of course, replace the need for a sufficiently large conventional force. A well-equipped conventional army to confront the present Soviet forces is still the best proof of the determination of the Western Alliance to defend itself.

This is why the presence of the U. S. Seventh Army in Germany is so highly important as a backbone of conventional defense. But there are more reasons. The army is, as I have already mentioned, an unmistakable token of American engagement in Europe. Furthermore, since these forces are also equipped with tactical nuclear weapons, the deterrent effectiveness provided by a possible early use of these weapons is evident. Finally, the experience which the commanders of the American army and the American officers in SHAPE acquire on the spot gives them a much deeper insight into the logic of our frontline military thinking—an insight that has quite often led to a cohesion of views between SACEUR and German military authorities— and, on the other hand, to some differences of opinion between SACEUR and the U. S. Department of Defense.

These are some of the bases for our belief that the NATO Alliance is indispensable to German national security. We are able and willing to make our own substantial contribution to the common defense effort. Recently it was reported that the twelfth German division was ready for assignment to NATO.

That all our national military forces are assigned to NATO is a unique phenomenon. It makes the German contingent the largest under NATO command. At the same time it results in the complete non-existence of an independent national German army. There is no German general staff, neither in peacetime nor in the case of war. There are no plans for a separate use of German forces for the defense of German territory. The German defense effort is entirely integrated in NATO.

We believe very strongly in the values of this integration, and for a number of good reasons. In the present day, military planning to prevent war must be co-ordinated, and the preparation for eventual defense must be as far ad-

vanced as possible. This makes it necessary to have even
in peacetime integrated staffs ready not only to take over
command of the armies of the Alliance on the first day of
an alert, but also to prepare today for all possible contingencies tomorrow. The integration of the staff structure
is a prerequisite for well-balanced common planning. What
is to the advantage of the Alliance as a whole can more
easily be worked out by an integrated body than by a
number of individual national general staffs. An integrated
staff, as we know, for example, from SACEUR, has a tendency to develop a thinking of its own. The close co-operation of staff officers from all the allied countries results, as
has been shown, in a meeting of minds which represents
much better thinking of the Alliance than an endeavor to
co-ordinate a number of different national war plans.

When the Federal Government advocates integration in
the defense field, it does so not only because of the size
of the possible threat and the necessity of displaying to our
opponents, before any aggression has been launched, the
highest military efficiency that can be provided and af-
forded, but also because of the need to indicate our readiness to participate in the common effort—a readiness that
can be understood against the background of a problem
that is essentially a consequence of Germany's political situation, past and present.

In being urged to fulfill its NATO force goals Germany
has, as I mentioned earlier, recently committed to NATO
her twelfth division. German forces now constitute the
largest army having modern equipment in Europe outside
the Soviet Union and still Germany is being urged to

continue the buildup, even as she tries to point out the tremendous difficulties which she faces in the fields of economics and manpower. In present-day Europe, however, a large German army inevitably is bound to originate political problems of every shade and magnitude. Let me mention just a few of them.

The nations of eastern Europe which have suffered from World War II and especially those which have in its wake taken possession of German territory, Poland and the Soviet Union, are quite understandably nervous, suspicious, even afraid of a large German national army. This can have adverse effects on the political developments in Europe and, above all, on the primary political objective of the Federal Republic—German reunification. Even though we believe that a strong and credible defense posture on the part of the West is the best way to dissuade the East from any idea of pursuing a policy of risks and from any hope for future openings in the Western defense belt, we recognize at the same time that a highly negative effect would result if the image of the West were interpreted as aggressive. The nations of eastern Europe would meld together rather than continue in the present development toward a growing disintegration of the Soviet bloc. The decentralization of the political system of the East together with an expanding feeling of national safety and security may very probably be the only way to achieve a political climate which would allow a kind of European arrangement in which the reunification of Germany would be the central piece.

Too strong a national German army might therefore very well be detrimental to our interest in reunification. It might also have ill effects on the political scene of western

Europe. The weight which the Federal Republic already has in manpower and economic strength would be accentuated by a national army—and if, as is now happening, the pace of the movement toward European integration slows down, the old pattern of distrust and rivalry, which has agitated the Continent for so many centuries, might possibly reappear. Moreover, we Germans wish to avoid internally the resurgence of a nationalistic Germany and hope instead for a further development of common European bonds.

Consequently, we have been prompted to ask for two things in order to make our participation in the defense of the West as safe as possible. We have accepted under the treaty of the Western European Union a system of arms control which was mainly designed to supervise the existing German armaments and the compliance of the Federal Republic in undertaking not to produce atomic-bacteriological-chemical (ABC) weapons and a specified group of other arms. Many of these limitations are clearly outdated— as, for instance, those on the size of warships.

We have accepted all this in recognition of the problems which German rearmament was bound to create, and we are willing to keep our word, even though, as I mentioned, some of the restrictions are archaic and lack equality.[1] I am somewhat reluctant to say that, in my opinion, there

---

[1] Article 3 of the protocol No. III on the control of armaments, for instance, provides: "When the development of atomic, biological and chemical weapons in the territory of the mainland of Europe of the High Contracting Parties who have not given up the right to produce them has passed the experimental stage and effective production of them has started there the level of stocks that the High Contracting Parties concerned will be allowed to hold on the mainland of Europe shall be decided by a majority vote of the Council of Western European Union."

should at least be equality among the allies in their seriousness in fulfilling their respective commitments.

More than by inequality in the field of control of armaments we are puzzled by an embarrasing animosity toward
integration inside NATO, which is currently pronounced by
our French friends. What the French reasons are can easily
be understood, for they are sound and logical: integration,
one believes, takes the patriotic fighting spirit out of the
army; it also deprives the nation of its freedom of decision
in matters of life and death. The De Gaulle formula for
military co-operation in peacetime, therefore, comes much
closer to the classical type of alliance than to the present
partly integrated NATO concept.

After what has been said previously, it is not hard to
imagine how worried we are about such an anti-integration
attitude. What will the consequences be if the concepts of
national armies and national strategies finally prevail?
General Ailleret wrote recently in the *Révue de la défense
nationale*: " . . . The Alliance can and must have a strategy. However, it cannot pretend to meet in the future all
the defense necessities of every member. Since there is still
a system of sovereign nations, national strategy has priority
over the strategy of the Alliance. From this national strategy
derives participation in the Alliance, which can therefore
only last as long as there arise no serious conflicts between
national strategy and that of the Alliance."

General Ailleret's warning voice, of course, is realistic.
Germany more than most of the other NATO countries is
experiencing the divergencies which arise in the process
of developing a common strategy for the Alliance between
national defense interests and those of the Alliance. What
are the conclusions which should be drawn from the reali-

zation of these natural tensions? In my opinion, everything should be done to prevent the serious conflicts mentioned by General Ailleret by working out a truly well-balanced strategy for the Alliance and, at the same time, by promoting on the national level as much understanding as possible of the values and necessities of common defense. The higher the degree of integration on the staff level, the easier this task will be. The more integration is impeded or cut back, the greater grows the danger of paralyzing if not divisive conflicts.

Our basic consideration is the overwhelming necessity of the Atlantic Alliance for Germany's defense. There is no European combination which could equal the protection offered by the Alliance to its members, and there is no acceptable substitute for it. It would be dangerous foolishness to run the risk of dissolving—or even weakening—NATO.

It has been argued that our insistence on the indispensability of Atlantic defense integration is dangerous because of a possible curtailment of the independence of individual nations to the advantage of the United States, and that furthermore, it is even unnecessary because the United States would have to defend Europe anyway. Neither argument is justifiable, at least from the German point of view. Aside from pre-eminent interest in integration for special German reasons, we have learned from experience that teamwork between America and Germany is not a one-way street. It has frequently also led to American understanding and even acceptance of German opinions and practices. Since we must face up to our dependence on the United States in matters of European defense, it is preferable that the nations to be defended have a seat in the cockpit rather than wait and guess whether and when support will come. And after all—even if it is certainly true at the present time that it is in the interest of the United States to accept high risk in order to prevent a Soviet attack on Europe—there is no reason why this should always be so. There is no such thing as a permanent identity of interests among different individual nations. By strengthening the Alliance and fostering integration within, we hope to develop an institution more durable and reliable than that provided by the classical type of alliance which our French friends seem to have in mind.

Obviously the Federal Republic here faces a dilemma. What is to be done if France cannot be convinced of the soundness and value of our arguments? A bilateral German-American arrangement that would transcend the present amount and scope of co-operation would probably not be a sound solution. It might indeed prove divisive for Europe and for the Atlantic system. A European solution, the extension of the European communities into the field of defense, would meet the specific German interest in integration even though restricted to a limited area. Unfortunately the prospects in this direction seem not too bright. The original attempt to establish a European Defense Community (EDC) among the Six failed when France decided not to ratify the treaty even after all the other instruments of ratification had been deposited in Paris. In his press conference of February 4, 1965, General de Gaulle called on the Six to "organize themselves in the fields of policy and defense." But we shall have to wait for concrete proposals. Ominously enough, the word "integration" has been replaced by "organization." The Western European Union which—with the inclusion of England

—would open the possibilities of more co-operation in the military and political field beyond the austere task of arms control, has been ineffective so far. Attempts to activate it have been quite unsuccessful, the problem of British relationship with the "Europe of the Six" obviously presenting additional obstacles.

As it now looks, the road to European political unity and military integration will be a very long one. The problem is emphasized by the fact that France today speaks of European unity—without committing herself to any form or principle for organizing this union. But even if we could some day arrive at a European Union, one which would be based on a certain amount of integration, the question remains as to what the relationship of this Europe with the Atlantic partners would be. It seems to me that the principle of tightly integrated common North Atlantic defense would also be applicable in the case of a European union—because the fate of Europe will depend for the foreseeable future on a close connection with the United States. Maybe there will be different levels of integration—a tighter European and a looser Atlantic level— but to let the Atlantic partnership be reduced to a mere traditional alliance would spell danger rather than progress in the realm of common defense. The possibility of future divergencies of interest might then even be increased by the appearance of a United Europe. The two big partners of the Atlantic system might slowly drift apart. Therefore, I believe that strong institutional links on the basis of integration ought to be maintained and expanded, even in the case of future European unity. It may well be that our French friends and allies as well will overcome their repugnance toward integration in an Atlantic framework once there exists a possibility of a "meaningful discussion" across the ocean on an equal basis.

An important factor determining the German attitude toward NATO and its development is the nuclear problem. Although as a conventional land power Germany is the second strongest contributor to the common defense effort, she is not a nuclear power, in contrast to the United States, Great Britain, and France. She has, as has been mentioned before, renounced the production of nuclear weapons on her territory and in addition has accepted a system of special "negative controls" under the WEU "Protocol on Control of Armaments." This commitment, which was part and parcel of the complex treaty system accompanying Germany's admission to NATO, is a very serious matter for the Federal Republic. An amendment to this undertaking is not and never has been considered. In our geographical position it is not possible, as it is in France, to cut to the bone the conventional forces in order to buy at least a limited nuclear deterrence. Above all, Germany is aware that she is still a nation with very pressing and real problems: the questions of reunification and a peace settlement. National nuclear weapons for the Federal Republic would hardly enable us to move closer toward these, our national aims.

But if the German attitude toward nuclear defense weapons coincides with the idea of non-proliferation and also with some specific national interests, it leaves open— if indeed it does not create—other problems. It leaves Germany entirely and absolutely dependent on the United States. It has been suggested in the first part of this paper that the best way to overcome the negative effects deriving

from this one-sided dependence is a close integration of
the Atlantic defense system. But this integration, relatively
easy as it may seem in the conventional field, proves tremendously difficult as soon as it shifts to nuclear weapons.
I do not wish to embark upon a close study of the reasons
for this phenomenon. We have to face the fact that for a
long time—and practically still today—the United States
is unwilling to share the final responsibility in the nuclear
field with other allies, obviously because it is deemed impossible to let other nations interfere with decisions involv-
ing the existence of the nation. On the other hand, it is
expected that other nations accept the thesis of the necessity of a United States veto as something inevitable and
natural. This self-contradictory attitude has been accentuated by the American effort to prevent proliferation of nuclear weapons, which led to opposition against the emergence of new nuclear power inside the Alliance and to a
policy of reducing the number of nuclear partners. As far
as the Alliance is concerned, this has meant perpetuation
of American hegemony, a simultaneous continuously
smoldering crisis of confidence, and, finally, a very possible
degeneration in the will and ability of the other allies for
self-defense. France has drawn conclusions and produced
her own nuclear weapons. Her example cannot be followed
by the Federal Republic for the reasons already explained.
To Germany the French action has had a double effect:
it has made things worse within the Alliance, for two
classes of nations are now definitely emerging—the nuclear and the non-nuclear allies. The nuclear allies have
their own and entirely independent—if sometimes small—
nuclear forces outside NATO. They can have a fuller self-
confidence, since they do not depend in the functioning of

nuclear deterrence entirely on the United States; the effectiveness of their small deterrent is augmented by the big U.S. nuclear power—whether the U.S. likes it or not. This position of the "nuclear allies" cannot but lead to a closer co-operation among them, and will possibly not be without consequences in international relations outside NATO; it is bound to create a split inside NATO by deepening the predicament of the non-nuclear nations. On the other hand, France's step was a lesson to American statesmen. It made clear that there existed a serious problem; and very soon after it was taken American policy-makers tried to apply the concept of integration to the nuclear field also. They did so not only in order to prevent the emergence of additional nuclear powers, but also—and, I believe, primarily—in order to try to repair the miscalculations that led to France's decision, and with some hope that Great Britain and France would eventually be induced to abolish their own national forces.

As could be anticipated, the Federal Republic backed fully the American proposal of a mixed-manned multilateral Polaris fleet, since the principle of integration that was used here as an approach to a solution to the nuclear problem in the Alliance was, at the same time, likely to introduce additional bonds of Western co-operation. If the proposal suffered setbacks, it was for a variety of reasons.

The idea of sharing control with non-nuclear powers—or, at least, a step in this direction—met with resistance in the U.S. Congress, which still strictly adheres to quite an uncompromising doctrine of non-proliferation. It did not arouse very much interest among the smaller states, especially Norway and Denmark, which traditionally steer a more neutralist course and which, in any event, because of their size, have to rely absolutely on American defense. It finally encountered the opposition of France, which, ironically, claimed that an integrated nuclear solution would split up the Alliance. It was further argued that the solution was a digression from the European path and, finally, that any kind of nuclear sharing by the Federal Republic would render reunification impossible.

Since France has not proposed an alternative European solution, it is quite obvious that she considers the present dichotomy of nuclear and non-nuclear nations the preferable status for the Alliance. Unfortunately, from the German point of view, it looks quite different. For us—and also for our Italian, Dutch, and Belgian friends (in short, the rest of the Six, if I may be permitted for a moment to neglect Luxembourg)—the nuclear problem in the Alliance is far from settled. And, as President Johnson's Georgetown speech has proven, the American government is well aware of this and is willing to co-operate. It may well be that the British version of the MLF idea, the ANF, will bring a solution. I regret to say that I do not see much hope for General Norstad's alternative proposals: There is not the slightest indication that France would be willing to put its *force de frappe* irrevocably into a NATO nuclear pool. Furthermore, the non-nuclear powers will hardly be satisfied with the concept of "irrevocably assigned" national nuclear forces. There is no irrevocability in political life. Finally, Norstad's idea smacks of the three-power nuclear directorate, of a course which would indeed be likely to break up not only the Atlantic Alliance but also European unity. This is not the time for some powers of the Alliance to aspire to a preponderant position; everybody should try to the best of his abilities to co-operate in the common undertaking of the integrated defense of the Atlantic area.

Finally, one word about the French assertion that German participation in the MLF would make reunification impossible. Gromyko, who stated the same view, was asked in New York whether reunification would become easier through non-participation of Germany in the MLF. His answer was a flat no. This confirms our impression that a nuclear sharing with the Federal Republic in the Atlantic framework would not work against our main political goal, reunification. However, I believe it is in keeping with the subject of this paper to ask, at least, how reunification will affect NATO. This question is not easy to answer. We cannot foresee the developments which will some day lead to German unity. If reunification should result from a general settlement of the European security problem, it might well be that NATO, as well as the Warsaw Pact, would be affected. But we do not see how such a European security system might look and what the role of either the Soviet Union or the U. S. would be in this context. This, however, is a look into an uncertain future, a future, though, which has to do with the main problems of a major NATO ally, Germany. For the time being and for the foreseeable future, the only thing we can do is to strengthen the Alliance, and this, I can assure you, is the well-considered policy of the Federal Republic of Germany.

Jens Boyesen

Contributions of Small Powers to the Alliance

THE TERM "small power" may call for a definition. It is difficult to give, except in a negative sense. In the simplest terms of physical force, there are still only two really great powers in the world—the United States and the Soviet Union. But in view of their histories and traditions, population, and economic strength, it would hardly occur to anyone to call countries like Britain and France—or Germany and Italy—small powers. For the purpose of the present discussion, then, the small countries can only be specified as the rest of the members of the Alliance.

The small powers in NATO have few characteristics in common. They range from Canada, with its vast territory and enormous economic potential, to Luxembourg, with its small territory and a population of only 350,000; from an island like Iceland, with its isolated position in the North Atlantic and no military establishment, to a country like Turkey, with a considerable military establishment and considerable regional influence. They include countries as different in background as Denmark and Norway, on the one hand, and Greece and Portugal, on the other.

To my mind, the conception of the smaller countries, having a special and to some extent joint role in international affairs is an out-dated one—if ever it had much reality. This idea was much in the foreground in the period between the two world wars. It acquired almost ideological and moralistic connotations, as though the small countries possessed some inherent virtue because of their smallness and absence of power. When Nazi aggression began in the 1930's, however, the illogic of such notions became clear; a number of small countries in Europe withdrew from even their limited collective-security obligations under the Covenant of the League of Nations. Certainly, during the fifteen years that NATO has now been in existence, differences in policy and approach have cut entirely across the line dividing the great from the small powers.

And yet there are some traits that the smaller members do have in common. An obvious one is that they all control real estate of great importance to the Alliance. The loss of any of their territories, from Greenland and the North Cape in the north to the Ararat in the southeast, would constitute a military catastrophe. The political defection of any of these countries would, particularly in times of tension or crisis, disastrously weaken the Alliance as a whole.

Another characteristic they have in common is a position within NATO which, formally speaking, is for out of proportion to their actual power in terms of population or economic or military strength. NATO is an alliance of sovereign nations; decisions can only be made by the concurrence of all.

In the early days of NATO, it was often said, particularly by the supporters of federalism in Europe, that NATO could operate with fifteen sovereign members because there was one member, the United States, which was so overwhelmingly stronger than the other countries that they were so dependent on its protection that they would adapt their policies accordingly. So in a sense the United States represented what otherwise might have been the role of a supranational body in the Alliance. Though there may have been something to be said for that point of view, it was soon found that the small countries who benefited from the protection of the United States were nonetheless still faced with all the risks of having to go to war in case of aggression against any one of the partners. This being the case, it was obviously unsatisfactory for any small country not to have a say in policies designed to meet challenges from the other side which might lead to a fatal crisis.

The question may well be asked whether an alliance with fifteen vetos can operate effectively at all. Does the presence of so many smaller countries make it unduly difficult to arrive at joint decisions? As I see it, the problem of the veto power is not so much related to the smaller members as it is to the major powers. For a small country, the right to prevent a decision which is desired by all or many of its partners is a very untempting tool. It is much easier to go against a proposal when you know that your negative vote merely indicates minority dissent than when you know that the position you take is decisive. For countries

holding great economic or military power and responsibility of the veto is, therefore, much more of a reality.

In any case, the NATO Council does not, on the whole,
operate primarily by way of hard and fast decisions. Most
of the specific resolutions which have been adopted deal
with practical and financial questions related to joint defenses such as infrastructure, command arrangements, etc.
When it comes to more general matters, the Council works
by way of discussion, trying to map out areas of agreement,
to identify where one can proceed, and to halt where there
are obviously no prospects of reaching agreement. Particularly in the political field, consultations have usually
not (though there are some exceptions) aimed at specific
resolutions. Rather the purpose has usually been to reach
a general meeting of minds or, at least, to clarify the
various positions so as to avoid unnecessary misunder-
standing. It is curious to note now, after regular political
consultation has been practiced for more than a dozen
years, that this type of permanent co-operation was not
envisaged in the North Atlantic Treaty. The Treaty only
provided—in Article 4—for consultation in case of emergency.

These permanent political consultations, which have
been common practice for years, have usually not, I believe, been rendered more unmanageable or less constructive by the participation of a number of small countries.
Quite the contrary, there is hardly any evidence that, when
the initial positions of the major powers differ, they find
it easier to reach agreement by themselves than in the
presence of smaller allies. At the risk of generalizing a
bit too much, I would say that the smaller countries have
a tendency to seek for compromise when consultation might

otherwise be ended. Also, with a greater number of partners involved, a prevailing view within the Alliance is
often more easily established. And, for the smaller countries, the NATO Council presents a forum where we can
present our views in the presence of all our partners. In
these discussions, no one small power is isolated and alone.
In addition, this procedure has provided an invaluable
source of information which has brought closer the political
realities of the day.

Political consultation in NATO has until now been most
successful in dealing with problems connected with the
original and basic function of the Alliance—the prevention
of Soviet expansion in western Europe. There has been a
great deal of work on guidelines respecting a definition of
vital Western interests, on contingency planning with regard to what response should be used in meeting various
threats which might develop, and on our collective approach to the Soviet Union. There has also been a high
degree of consensus in regard to disarmament questions,
which, I believe, are directly linked to the basic functions
of NATO, though I do not think the NATO Council has
been particularly fertile in developing new ideas. But this
whole process of continuous policy consultation is a great
innovation in international affairs, certainly as between so
many and such varied countries. To illustrate my point, I
ask you to think back to the early 1920's and to contem-
plate what the reaction would have been if the foreign
secretary of Great Britain, in all his aristocratic and power-
conscious position, had been asked, before sending a note
to Russia, to present it for critical examination to countries such as Luxembourg, Norway, and Greece. Yet just
this procedure has now become almost a matter of course

in NATO, though, we must confess, less so recently than some years ago.

It would be false to assume that NATO consultation has been equally successful in dealing with problems and crises on other continents or with the "North-South" problem in general (which NATO is neither well equipped nor politically well placed to deal with anyway). It is apparent that the major powers, with their different degrees of involvement in various sections of other continents, have not to any striking extent developed common policies themselves. It may be that the presence of the small members has made it even more difficult to begin effective consultations on African, Asian, or Latin American problems which are, indirectly in any case, of concern to everybody.

There are differing views among the smaller countries on how far to go in trying to concert policy on "extraneous" matters within NATO. It is generally recognized that putting geographical limitations upon political consultation is artificial. On the other hand, some governments—the Scandinavian ones among them—have felt that there must be some reasonable limitation upon the responsibilities and commitments which small countries can reasonably undertake as a consequence of NATO membership.

We have no independent source of information necessary to evaluate different situations; we do not have the resources. It is not natural for us to be involved in every critical situation which may arise. Viet Nam is a case in point. We have been somewhat reticent to discuss that area from the time the French began to experience difficulties in holding their former colony. In recent days, we have hesitated to discuss United States policy there, not because of any lack of understanding of, or sympathy with, the terrible American responsibilities there, which are not the result of their own choice but arise from their position in the world.

Furthermore, while we want as much harmony as possible among the NATO countries, there are certain advantages in a more individual approach to problems outside the NATO area. Certainly, in the United Nations, it would be self-defeating to try to operate as a political bloc. Such a procedure would be wide open to the charge of neo-colonialism, and we might well add to each other's difficulties rather than help toward their solution. On the other hand, various NATO countries may be more effective in exerting influence individually in situations arising in Africa and Asia through their historical ties with the countries in those parts of the world.

The relative lack of success that NATO has had in dealing with world-wide matters is no reason to feel despondent over the state of the Alliance, however. NATO was not created to cure all the ills of the world. The crisis within NATO—crisis in the sense that some basic problems remain unresolved—has rather to do with *internal* problems within the Alliance. It relates to such matters as the relative roles of North America and western Europe, how to share or apportion atomic responsibility and political influence, and how to find a balance between independent national action and allied solidarity.

While the small countries can and do take a detached position on these issues, we recognize that the problem is more acute for major countries with greater power and different historical traditions. It has, of course, been the French who have most frequently expressed dissatisfaction. They look upon the large degree of military integration that has been reached as something contrary to the historical needs of the European members of the Alliance. They feel that to be effective military forces must to the maximum extent possible draw upon national interest and national emotion. I think that in this particular respect most, if not all, the allies disagree with our French friends. A primary controversy has developed around the problem of nuclear responsibility. For the last four or five years, a search has been made for new and better ways to devise a common nuclear strategy. Again our French friends have taken a more extreme stand than other members of the Alliance. They feel, first, that France must have its own nuclear capability. Though, as far as I know, they have not officially questioned the United States guarantee to Europe, they seem to think the more vulnerable the United States becomes to the Russian nuclear force, the more there is a need for an independent French and European capability.

On this issue, there is a basic difference of opinion among members of the Alliance. The French nuclear force is a fact, and I think, an irreversible one. Though some eminent statesmen in Europe disagree with me, I myself am not sure that there is a need for a rearrangement within the Alliance of responsibilities in the nuclear field. While the existence of such a group is asserted in diplomatic and political circles, I myself have never met those Europeans who are supposed to feel anxious that the United States might not fully commit herself in case of aggression in Europe. Rather did the course of the MLF negotiations indicate that when the moment approaches for a decision to change the present arrangement, there is, in fact, great hesitancy to do so on the part of the European countries, both large and small.

Any argument that the United States guarantee to Europe is less valid today than it was earlier is refuted in NATO defense-planning and, what is more important, in the realities of the American military posture, specifically in the presence of American military forces in Europe. I accept Secretary of State Dean Rusk's statement that the American guarantee to Europe in general, and in regard to atomic matters in particular, is neither verbal nor written into treaty clauses, but is a physical fact by reason of the presence of 400,000 American troops in Europe.

Another argument which has been raised in support of changing the present arrangements is that if something is not done to bring all—or at least some—of the European countries more firmly into nuclear decision-making, it would be difficult to avoid a national nuclear development in Germany. To my mind, this is a myth, since it accords neither with the intentions of German politicians and parties nor with the mood of the German people. In addition, the Federal Republic of Germany has treaty commitments which it could hardly break without undermining the whole Alliance and, thereby, its own security.

Much has been said about the difference in points of view held by the members of the Alliance, but not much damage has been done by airing those differences. Amid the clamor of dispute over nuclear matters, one should not overlook the progress made over the last six or seven years. Almost every year, another step has been taken until we have now reached the point that European officers from a number of countries take part in the planning at the strategic commands. In my opinion, this problem of sharing influence and responsibility is not so much an

American-European problem as it is a European one. We do not know what the course of European developments will be over the next, say, five years; and I cannot see any justification for basic innovations until we can at least dimly discern those developments.

In recent French pronouncements, the idea has been suggested of making a distinction between the Atlantic Alliance as such and NATO as an organization, the implication being, if I understand correctly, that the former continues to be a useful treaty arrangement, whereas the latter is a passing phenomenon ill adapted to the changing conditions of the 1960's. Here, I believe, is a point about which all small countries feel great concern. If the Alliance should cease to have day-to-day reality as a practical system of military and political co-operation and become a mere set of verbal guarantees, the rest being left to big-power diplomacy and arrangements—in that case, public opinion in many countries might become opposed to taking the risks that are necessarily involved in any allied partnership.

A fundamental problem in NATO—as, indeed, in any Alliance of many countries—is how to handle emergencies. When decisions have to be made quickly, one cannot wait for the fifteenth government to make up its mind, nor expect communications to function effectively all around. Would a directorate composed of representatives of the principal powers serve to solve this problem?

There have been two different conceptions of such a directorate. The first prescribes a body made up of representatives of the nuclear powers within the Alliance, with, perhaps, a rotating member from one of the other NATO countries, which would have responsibility for making decisions on the use of nuclear weapons; the second, a somewhat larger directorate, charged with performing more general political functions. To my mind, both ideas are unrealistic.

It is obvious that if ever the decision to use nuclear weapons has to be made, only a minimum of consultation will be feasible. The decision will have to be made by whoever has the requisite power and position—and this means, ultimately, the President of the United States. This we all accept as a fact of life. It is something entirely different formally to delegate authority to a group of foreign governments to make decisions on one's own behalf which may involve the very existence of all the allied nations, even if a way could be devised constitutionally to do this.

A general directorate made up of five powers or thereabout would leave the rest somewhat resentful and would formalize a sort of caste system within the Alliance. It is by no means obvious that there are many problems of more particular concern to such a group than to others, nor that many decisions they might make would not directly touch the interests of other members. In an emergency, many of the same problems of consultation that exist in NATO would arise within the smaller group. Besides, there is nothing in NATO to prevent any group of countries from engaging informally in specific co-operative enterprises and establishing any diplomatic contact that they may desire.

Since widespread consultation may admittedly prove unrealistic and the smaller countries, in particular, cannot expect to exercise any effective influence once an emergency arises, could more advance planning, not only in the military but also in the political field, meet expressed concerns? The argument is used (here I think it is a valid one) that whereas we may have a great deal of co-operation and consultation in normal periods, this would break down in emergencies if for no other reasons than the aforementioned difficulty in communications. In such critical emergencies, say, as the Cuban crisis, it is very difficult to consult fifteen governments, or even five. Thus there is general agreement in NATO that we must go as far as possible in planning in advance possible steps to meet problems with which we may be faced. This contingency planning has been quite successful with respect to Berlin; in theory, at least, all the NATO governments have participated to some degree in the establishment of certain guidelines for responses to possible threats and challenges. We also established in 1961 some guidelines with respect to the use of nuclear weapons, but these are limited to obvious situations. Actually, NATO contingency planning cannot proceed very far. Moreover, since the future cannot be accurately foreseen, too rigid advance planning may limit the exercise of free judgment in a critical situation. A departure from plans agreed upon by many nations, even if only tentatively undertaken, may easily become an irrational factor producing dispute in an already complicated situation. It is the unobvious contingencies which may be the most dangerous, and over-planning may, indeed, weaken the structure of deterrence. The Soviet side has pretty good information on what is going on at NATO. It is necessary not to hand out recipes on what plans exist and how far they can safely go.

What I have said is no argument against trying whenever possible to work out common principles and identify vital common interests. But ultimately an alliance of free countries must rest upon confidence and not the least so in emergencies.

It may be asked whether present international trends do not lead away from the group or bloc which has been the objective of NATO. Nationalism seems to be a resurgent force, certainly in the developing countries. The same phenomenon can be seen, and in a most positive way, in eastern Europe, where the countries which used to be complete Soviet satellites are gradually—and within limitations—trying to reassert their own national identities. Nor has the Western Alliance itself been immune from independent national actions. Now, this world-wide development may be useful up to a point. In the United Nations, for example, many countries can be more effective when operating individually than as components of a bloc. But as far as the Western Alliance is concerned, independent, individual policy should not be carried so far as to endanger basic solidarity. If we should ever return to a situation in which we faced a resurgence of the national rivalries which have been the curse of Europe for centuries and centuries, it would be a tragedy. What we gained after the war in NATO and other organizations is a more civilized way of dealing with international rivalries. For small countries—but for all countries large and small it likewise holds true—it is obvious that no lasting solutions to our fundamental problems can be found by each alone.

We in the West have no interest in breaking up the basic security arrangements on the Eastern side. If the trend toward a loosening of Soviet ties reaches the point that basic Russian interests are affected and if we participate too actively and obviously in this process of loosening, we might well make it impossible for any Soviet government to pursue a moderate policy. We might, in fact, present the Russians with temptations which they would have difficulty in resisting. Patience, on the other hand, may encourage equal patience on the part of the Communists, who believe, after all, that our form of society is bound to fail ultimately. Basic solidarity, finally, is necessary to the policy of détente and the search for mutual accommodation since it is between the *group* of the West and the *group* of the East that agreement may best be arranged. The validity of the group—which paves the way, perhaps, for a more universal approach—is not disputed in the economic field; it is no less obvious an approach in the security field. In seeking agreements in this area, the approach, while taking into account the interests of individual countries, must be a joint one. No lasting accords can be negotiated by the few behind the backs of the others, even though they separately dispose of no great power.

I would like to say a few words about my own country, Norway. When we joined NATO in 1949, it was nothing less than a revolution in our foreign policy. Many commentators at the time took considerable exception to our membership. They felt that it was too provocative to the Soviet Union to bring into the new Western military system a bordering country which was also part of traditionally neutral Scandinavia. But as the situation had developed in Europe after the war, the Norwegian government could see no other alternative to safeguard our security, and it was supported in this view by an overwhelming majority in Parliament. In order to counteract suspicion or misgivings in the Soviet Union, in neighboring countries, at home, or elsewhere, we made a unilateral declaration at the time to the effect that bases would not be opened to foreign forces unless we felt threatened by war. This policy we have since maintained, and we believe that it has served to stabilize the situation in northern Europe. Along the same line, nuclear warheads are not stored on Norwegian territory. The Danish government has followed a similar policy.

Within these limitations, which, we believe, are in accord with general allied interests, we participate fully in the joint NATO defense system. Nearly all our forces are earmarked for NATO command; extensive allied infrastructure facilities have been built in Norway, and regular allied exercises are held.

There is a particularly strong political feeling in Norway—expressed in government and by the public alike—that nothing in our NATO policy should run contrary to our desire to see and our efforts toward a strengthening of the United Nations. There is nothing original about this, and we have no illusions about the present capacities of the U. N., but this sentiment regarding the general international organization is particularly strong in Norway —as, indeed, it is in all of Scandinavia.

That having been said, we continue to believe that what President Kennedy called the "Grand Design" remains a constructive set of ideas to guide Western policy. On both sides of the Atlantic, it calls for a breaking down of barriers, both political and economic. In Europe, it calls for political and economic consolidation, with the full participation of Great Britain and other countries not now members of the Six. In the rest of the world, it calls for an outward-looking, not narrowly introspective, approach.

Evelyn Shuckburgh

Great Britain and the Western Alliance

BRITAIN is a country which has had to undertake a drastic readjustment of its role in the world. Unlike some other countries, which have been forced to make similar readjustments by defeat in war or by enemy occupation, we have had to do it in the aftermath of two wars in which we have been on the winning side. We have had to reassess ourselves of our own volition, so to speak, and by forcing ourselves to admit unpleasant facts which it would have been more agreeable to overlook. We have had to make a conscious readjustment—I do not say that it has been voluntary, for no nation draws in its horns voluntarily—but a conscious one, because the reduction of British power and the change in the whole character of our position in the world have been caused by deep and not wholly visible trends over which we have had little control. It is in some ways easier for a nation to adjust itself to defeat than for a people who have had a great empire and world-wide connections and influences to accept the reduction of their status with a good grace and in good order when there is no irrefutable, tangible proof that they have got to do so.

We have been undergoing an immense readjustment in our national life both externally and internally. We have practically completed the task of launching our former colonies and dependencies into independence, thereby launching them on a sea which has proved rather rougher than some of us thought it might be. Almost all of them have chosen to remain within the Commonwealth, and we find this a very gratifying fact. It is a very different sort of Commonwealth from what we knew before the war. But it is nonetheless an important association. We feel that it has an important part to play in the world, being a voluntary grouping of nations, European, African, and Asian, which bridges the great racial gulfs that threaten so ominously to divide humanity in this century. The Commonwealth has no central machinery, no secretariat, no rules. Nevertheless, it works in the sense that its leaders meet one another frequently, exchange views on all the problems of the day and share a common respect for the Queen as Head of the Commonwealth. What exactly will be the practical role of the Commonwealth in the future, how effectively its members can work together, is still to be proved. How much importance to attach to it is one of the controversial questions which preoccupy those in Britain who are thinking about the shape of our future

foreign policy. As you know, the recently elected Labor
government in England places perhaps more emphasis
on the Commonwealth connection in relation to our other
connections than the previous government did. One hard
fact which we have to remember is that 40 per cent of
our food imports into the United Kingdom comes from
Commonwealth countries. Our foreign aid goes mainly to
Commonwealth countries.

Nor have we yet resolved, either in practice or in our
own minds, the question of what sort of nation we ourselves want to be, what part we want to play in the
world, and how much weight we can expect to exercise,
in the light of our economic and political character. Does
Britain have to choose between being, on the one hand, a
European country like other western European countries,
merging itself gradually into a European union, or, on the
other hand, an off-shore island with an overseas destiny,
primarily interested in the Commonwealth, its trade, and
its relationships around the world? The truth is that both
potentialities exist side by side in our national character
and situation, and that they are not incompatible. The
question is in what proportions should they weigh in the
scale when we make decisions about our future. I think
myself that today and in the coming years our European
connection needs special emphasis and attention, largely
because it has been under-stressed by us for nearly a
century. In the heyday of the British Empire, that is, up
to and including the lives of most of our fathers, British
thoughts and affections were led away from Europe toward
the glittering opportunities and responsibilities that were
open to our people in far parts of the world. Young men
from the British Isles who wanted adventure, travel, serv-

ice, or responsibility beyond their own doorsteps, poured out across the oceans onto every continent. They joined the army or the navy or the Colonial Service or the great trading companies; they served in India, in the Middle East, in the Far East, where work was to be done, exciting lives to be led, and often money to be made. Europe may have been on their doorstep, but the horizons that attracted their ambition lay far beyond. I remember being told when I was a boy how many of the letters delivered every morning in an average English postal district came from beyond the oceans; it was staggering—something like 20 per cent. You could not find many families without a relative in the dominions, or sons or daughters who had served or were serving in far places. The British people knew about most parts of the world.

Much of this has changed. But it still retains a powerful influence over our thinking and our habits. The ebb tide of our nineteenth-century expansion has left behind great islands of English-speaking population with whom we retain family and familiar connections of all kinds: Canada, Australia, New Zealand, to say nothing of the strongly rooted English traditions and friendships which still remain in the Indian subcontinent, in South America, and in Africa. These connections can never be forgotten by a British government in formulating its policies for the future. But the young in Britain today no longer see before them quite that wide variety of openings for activity and service beyond the seas. If you joined the army in my father's day, the odds were that you went to India, you served in the mountains of Kashmir, or in Egypt; today you are more likely to go to Germany. The British people of today do travel abroad, as all islanders must, in enormous numbers. But for holidays and for study the Continent of Europe is the place that attracts the greatest numbers. Tourism now takes thousands of Englishmen every year into countries where French, Italian, German, and Spanish are spoken. Languages are taught much more intensively. Trade and commercial links are formed in Europe, and a new pattern begins to be set. Our economic stake in Europe is already very great, and it is growing.

Even so short a time ago as 1962, a larger proportion of our total exports went to the Commonwealth than to Europe. The figures were 35 and 32.6 per cent. In 1964, the figures were reversed, and we exported for the first time more to Europe (34.1 per cent compared with 33 per cent). Our imports follow the same pattern; that is to say, the European trade grows steadily in relation to the Commonwealth trade.

I believe it is inevitable that any British government of the future, whatever special preferences or prejudices it may have, will be forced to give a high priority to strengthening our ties with other European countries. It was a bad day for Britain and for Europe when our entry into the Common Market was prevented two years ago. It was bad for us because it was a defeat for the people in England who wanted our country to be more European-minded; and in some respects it was an encouragement to insularity. It was also bad for Europe because it set a wrong standard for what Europe ought to be and wants to be. We were excluded on the grounds that the British were not yet sufficiently "European," as if there was some sort of examination which we had not yet passed. But, in fact, our exclusion put a stop to the progress of Europe itself toward political unity. We do not think that there can possibly be a sane development of Europe without British participation, and the vast majority of Europeans agree with us.

But it would be a poor sort of Europe if the countries which make it up were expected to eliminate from their character all tendencies which were not European and to abandon their interests and commitments in other parts of the world. Now that for the first time for several hundred years Europe shows signs of being able to unite, the great question is whether this quality of diversity, of looking outward, will prevail or not. One cannot be sure; there are tendencies the other way. There is still much nationalism, much uncritical belief that one's own nation's prosperity and pride can cohabit with the poverty and discomfiture of its neighbors. There are also, even among the advocates of a united Europe, some who see it in terms of a new European nationalism, excluding and developing in conflict with the United States and other parts of the Free World.

The Europe that we want to join and that we want to make when we are able to get together with our Continental friends is of the other kind. In 1962, Mr. Dean Acheson said in a public speech that Britain had lost an empire and had not yet found a role. There is a great deal of truth in that, in my opinion, although it gave some offense in England at the time. But I think it is not the whole truth. I think the truth is that Europe has not yet found its role. And, since Britain is a part of Europe, it is quite impossible that Britain's future should be mapped out clearly while Europe's future is veiled in obscurity. Europe has not yet decided whether it is ready to merge national sovereignty in a larger unity or whether it will

allow itself to be divided into two Europes, as would be
the trend if the European Economic Community and the
Outer Group were allowed to drift apart. It has not decided whether it is to be an inward-looking, nationalistic
Europe, trying to adopt a Third Force position between
the United States and the Soviet Union, or whether, as
we British certainly hope, it will be a Europe international,
Atlantic-minded, co-operating with the United States and
Canada, and ready to play a constructive part in the search
for a genuine deterrent to Eastern aggression. A few years
ago, many people thought that the continental Europeans
had already chosen unity and that only the British were
hesitating. I think this is no longer so. The European vision
of Jean Monnet is now shadowed by the very different
vision of General de Gaulle. It is not now at all certain
that the Six can move on from the economic co-operation
which they have achieved to political unity. In our judgment, this requires a joint effort by all of western Europe,
including Britain, for we cannot and will not be left out.

Nations, of course, cannot decide suddenly to change
their character, and there is little realism in a policy which
demands that a nation "choose" between this or that alignment within the Free World of this century. Nations, like
individuals, can only try to be true to their own natures,
assess correctly their capabilities, and to set their course
of action accordingly.

I am going to speak about British defense policy, and
I have made this introduction in order to show why we
have a specially difficult problem rather different from
that of most other NATO countries in deciding where to
place the weight of our defense effort, how to distribute
the resources which we now command, limited as they

are compared with the past. In broadest terms, the claims on our effort can be divided into two: Europe, and what we call "East of Suez"; that is to say, our contribution to NATO and Atlantic defense, on the one hand, and the maintenance of our remaining responsibilities overseas, on the other.

We are a nation of approximately the same size in population, gross national product, and state of development as France and Western Germany. In terms of population alone we are about half the size of Japan. All these countries are keen competitors of ours in the international commercial markets. Yet when you look at the burdens we are carrying, you find that they are out of proportion to those borne by the countries I have mentioned. Germany and Japan have no defense responsibilities outside their own territories and quite rightly have no desire to acquire any; France outside Europe has, since the end of the Algerian war, had only some residual military commitments to her former African colonies, now independent states. But Britain is still obliged to maintain armed forces in no less than twenty places around the world outside Europe. These range from our large garrison in Singapore, recently reinforced for the protection of Malaysia, to the single guard ship which protects the Falkland Islands off the tip of the South American continent, or the small Royal Air Force detachment operating the strategic airfield at Gan, a coral island 400 miles southwest of Ceylon on the strategic route to the Far East.

Some of these commitments are the consequence of history—we still have to look after a number of scattered territories and populations which are too small or too poor to stand on their own—while others (for example, our bases in Singapore and the Indian Ocean, in Aden and British Guiana, and so on) are part and parcel of the Western defense position against communism and against aggression and subversion generally, throughout the world. At the present moment, our government is particularly conscious of the importance of these commitments, and is giving a certain priority to them. You will see that reflected in many of our recent decisions, such as that to reinforce Malaysia. This commitment results from the defense agreement between Britain and Malaya signed in 1957, when we undertook to help that newly established country with her external defense. In the face of Sukarno's "crush Malaysia" policy we are having to spend in the Far East about one-fifth of the operational part of our defense expenditure; and with the recent reinforcements we have more than 50,000 men in Malaysia, as well as powerful air and naval forces. Our situation there is also relevant to the forward defense of Australia and New Zealand and to our responsibilities to SEATO.

Unlike the Far East, we have in the Near East a national economic interest, namely to maintain the supply of oil on satisfactory terms. We think that these interests are best served by political stability in the area and by the maintenance of the major oil-producing Arab countries as independent, orderly states. Our judgment is that the military presence which we maintain in the Persian Gulf, notably the base at Aden, is an important factor in insuring the continuance of the equilibrium there and in containing communist, especially Soviet, penetration in the area. Middle East oil is not simply a British concern. Some two-thirds of the oil requirements of all western Europe are now met from the Middle East and North Africa, and this dependence is likely to continue despite the development of new sources of supply. If British companies were excluded from the Middle East, the additional annual cost to our balance of payments—already subject to severe strains—would probably be not less than £200 million. This, then, is the background for the presence of British troops in Aden, Bahrain, and the desert outposts and airfields of Sharjah and Masirah on the Persian Gulf. Because Britain has obligations in the Far East, we need to have the ability to get there and to reinforce our garrisons in emergency. This calls for staging posts on the way, and one of our main military objectives is to keep open military air communications across the Middle East land barrier so as to be able to reinforce our bases in the Middle East and Far East. We have an important staging post for our aircraft in Libya, with whom we also have a collective defense agreement. The sovereign base areas which we retain in Cyprus are a factor in our general military position in the Middle East and enable us to fulfill our obligations to CENTO; and it was because we had these bases that we found ourselves bearing the initial brunt of peace-keeping operations in Cyprus last year. We think that we must maintain these overseas responsibilities in the common interest, because these are things that nobody can do for us.

At the same time, we contribute to the defense of Europe, with a commitment to keep three divisions (about 55,000 men), backed by air forces, on the Continent in peacetime—a thing which we have never done in our history—which places a direct burden on our balance of payments to the tune of £85 million a year across the exchanges. All these British forces on the Continent are under integrated NATO command and would be immediately engaged in any hostilities. And, finally, we were in the nuclear business from the start too, with all that that implies in expenditure and in the use of technical manpower. No other nation of our size and standing is carrying all these three burdens at one and the same time.

It is always difficult to make fair and meaningful comparisons between the defense efforts of various countries. The best rough yardstick available is to compare the proportions of gross national products devoted to defense by each of them, but even this ignores important factors such as relative standards of living. The figures do not reflect, for example, the element of sacrifice involved for each country; a rich man can afford a private army and still eat well, but a poor man may have to go without a meal to equip himself with a cudgel. It is the same with nations. National income per head of population in the United States for 1963 was $2,490; for Turkey the figure was $189; and for the United Kingdom $1,252—exactly half that of the United States. These figures illustrate what I mean.

The British defense budget has for some years now taken about 7 per cent of our gross national product, and the current figure is 7.2 per cent. This is as much as we spend on equipping industry with plant and machinery, and nearly one and a half times what we spend on publicly financed education of all kinds. Defense now uses one-fifth of all the qualified scientists and technologists engaged on research in Britain, and it accounts for about 40 per cent of our research and development expenditure. The United States has been spending some 10 per cent, but this proportion is falling. (The President has recently announced a reduction of $300 million in this year's budget as compared with last year's.) The figures for France, Germany, and Italy are 6.6, 5.9, and 4.1 per cent; the Japanese spend about 1.5 per cent. As I have said, all these countries are competitors with us in the world markets. What it amounts to is that we are trying to maintain a very varied effort—in Europe, outside Europe, and in the nuclear field—at a time when economic and commercial considerations point to an urgent need for us to reduce our defense expenditures, or, at least, to keep them in bounds.

Therefore, our first concern in looking at the defense problem today is to avoid unnecessary expense and to make sure that we get value for our money. It is the same concern that lies behind Mr. McNamara's insistence on "cost-effectiveness" in your defense program. Modern armed forces and weapons have become so fantastically expensive that no one can afford duplication or waste. We are all in the same boat on that.

But there is another thing. Now that nuclear war has become something which cannot be fought without destroying the world, the total defense system of the NATO alliance must be judged primarily from the point of view of its deterrent effect and not from the point of view of winning a major war. This has forced us all to adopt an entirely new approach to the problem of selecting weapons-systems and deciding the shape of our forces, because it is quite obvious that what is required to deter aggression may be very different from what would be required for actually fighting a long war. To put it crudely, the weapons which are handed to soldiers nowadays are not necessarily the weapons which soldiers would choose for their tested value in the field. They are just as likely to be weapons which are considered by politicians, philosophers, and Kremlinologists to be likely to affect the enemy's intentions by the mere fact that we possess them. This introduces, I might point out, a new complexity in the relations between civilians and military men. And whereas in the past it was safe to assume that anyone who had a weapon would at once use it if he were attacked, today we have to think very hard about such questions as whether it is likely that the enemy will think it likely that we shall use certain weapons that we possess.

What are NATO's defense forces really for? Broadly speaking, they serve two political aims; they give confidence to us and they impose caution on the enemy. Our own confidence — speaking for the European allies — is based mainly on our knowledge of American strategic superiority. But it is also assured, and perhaps more directly, by the physical presence of soldiers and airmen from allied countries in or near the places where we live. This is certainly so in the case of populations living near the Iron Curtain or in exposed parts like northern Norway or Greece. This is one reason by the United States, Great Britain, France, and other countries keep troops in Germany, and it is also the reason why SACEUR's multinational Mobile Force is so important. This is quite a small force (not to be confused with the "Multilateral Force"!) designed to be sent a moment's notice to a threatened area, not as a reinforcement to help the local troops fight a war there, but rather to give proof to the enemy before he attacks that, if he attacks in that area, he will come up against soldiers of other allied countries and not only the soldiers of the country attacked. And the

exercises carried out in peacetime by SACEUR's Mobile
Force play, of course, a very large part in giving confidence to the armed forces of countries in those exposed
spots. The Mobile Force is, in effect, a symbol of the unity
of the Alliance, and it is the unity of the Alliance which
gives confidence to the member countries.

Establishing and keeping up an effective deterrent
system involves many new problems and raises many new
arguments. In order to be credible, the system must be
realistic and likely to work. And it is this consideration that
immediately brings up the argument over strategy, on which
so much heat is engendered within NATO. On one side is the
"trip wire" strategy, which would fire off everything if any
aggression, no matter how small, occurred (a strategy usually associated with the French), and on the other is the
strategy described as the "flexible response" (usually associated with United States military thinking).

British views on strategy are pretty close to the American in the sense that we agree that a threat to loose total
nuclear war in response to a limited, conventional aggression is simply not credible. But we also understand the
preoccupation of European countries, particularly those
which, like West Germany, would be the scene of a conventional attack. These countries are troubled by the
thought that a flexible strategy might be too flexible in that
it might, if followed too logically, allow long, conventional
battles to take place over their territory and even result
in a loss of a great part of their territory before the United
States authorized the use of the nuclear weapon. As an
illustration of European anxieties, I would cite a recent
article in *Foreign Affairs* by the German Defense Minister,
Herr von Hassel, in which he states that, while the Ger-

mans accept the American doctrine of a flexible response,
they are very concerned that a low threshold be kept between conventional and nuclear response.

These arguments over allied military strategy are intimately related to the problem of giving the non-nuclear
members a greater sense of participation in the control
of Alliance nuclear policy. I believe this major problem
will be with us for some time. No doubt the simplest division of responsibility among the NATO countries would be
for the United States to look after the whole of the nuclear side and for the European allies to provide conventional defense in the forward areas. There might be
a certain logic in this arrangement, but we also know that
it is impossible over the long run because it would place
the non-nuclear powers in a state of permanent inferiority.
Britain and France already have the capacity to establish
and maintain nuclear forces of their own, and other countries in the Alliance could acquire a similar capacity if
they put their minds to it. Rightly or wrongly, nuclear
power has come to be regarded as a status symbol. There
are three ways in which the problem could be overcome.
The first would be for additional European countries to
make and own nuclear forces of their own; the second
would be for European countries to pool their resources
and to create a European or third nuclear force; and the
third would be to find some means of sharing responsibility for and control over nuclear weapons within the
existing system in such a way as to create an adequate
sense of equality.

The first approach entails the proliferation of national
nuclear forces. Such a development would certainly create
a great obstacle to any effective détente or even to peace-

ful coexistence betwen East and West. In addition, I think
it is right to say that nuclear proliferation is contrary to
the deepest instincts of most of the world. Some think it
is inevitable: that in twenty years every country will have
a bomb. Nonetheless, all of us instinctively fear this "solution," and, at any rate, the United States, Great Britain,
and a number of other NATO countries are determined to
prevent proliferation if they can. For us in England, non-
dissemination of nuclear weapons is one of the principal
aims of our present foreign policy. While we had a long
start over all the other NATO countries, except the United
States, in the creation of nuclear power, we do not think
that our experience encourages the idea of independent,
national nuclear forces. We have reached the conclusion
that there are no foreseeable circumstances in which we
should want to use nuclear power in Europe independently of the over-all NATO strategic deterrent. As a direct
consequence, we are offering to put all our nuclear forces,
including the four Polaris submarines we are now building, into a common NATO pool, jointly owned and controlled. The plain fact is that the burden of maintaining
an up-to-date, credible nuclear arsenal and delivery system
is becoming well beyond the economic means of any country except the two largest—the United States and the
Soviet Union. We are quite sure that other countries,
including France, will be driven to the same conclusion
when the real difficulties are borne in on them.

Then there is the second approach—for Europe to have
its own nuclear forces. This would not be, in the technical sense, nuclear proliferation if the forces included the
British and the French national units and if the British
and the French retained their veto over the use of the

forces. But in political terms, this second approach would
tend to split the Alliance into two camps and perhaps
encourage the United States to withdraw from Europe
and concentrate her defense nearer home. And in military
terms, furthermore, it would be contrary to what we regard
as an axiom: that nuclear war is indivisible and that the
West should prepare for one nuclear conflict, not several or
a series of them. Most important of all, there exists no European political authority even among the Six, quite regardless of the British relationship, and there is not likely to be
in the near future an authority capable of owning and
controlling such a European force. Nonetheless, I personally feel that, if ever a politically united Europe were
to come into being and especially if Britain were a part
of it, it would develop within the framework of the Atlantic Alliance its own defense and have its own forces of all
types.

So we come down to the third solution, which is to
work out a system of sharing nuclear responsibility in
NATO which will satisfy the legitimate demands of the
non-nuclear countries to be more closely associated with
the nuclear deterrent and which, at the same time, will
not endanger the prospects for disarmament by creating
new centers of nuclear power. Various proposals to this
end have been put forward. They are of two kinds: institutional or multinational, on the one side, and multilateral,
on the other. An example of the first type is the "guidelines" which were approved by the NATO ministers in
Athens in 1962, setting forth the circumstances in which
nuclear weapons might be used and including certain
undertakings by the nuclear powers to consult their allies,
time and circumstances permitting, before using nuclear

weapons anywhere in the world. The same Athens meeting established a NATO nuclear committee, which really is the NATO Council sitting under stricter security arrangements, to act as the forum for the exchange and discussion of sensitive nuclear information.

A year ago, another institutional arrangement was adopted in Ottawa reorganizing all the nuclear weapons in Europe into what was called an "inter-allied nuclear force." The British V-bomber force was assigned to it, and a new deputy for nuclear affairs, a non-American, was appointed at SHAPE under the Supreme Allied Commander to be responsible to General Lemnitzer for the nuclear planning of his command. Also the number of European officers from SHAPE stationed in a liaison capacity at Omaha was increased, thereby giving more participation to non-nuclear countries in this American strategic-planning center.

The primary aim of all these steps was to give the non-nuclear countries a better understanding of the problems and responsibilities arising from the exercise of nuclear power. We thought at the time they were good arrangements, and I think they still are. But the fact is that they were not given time to have an effect. The ink was hardly dry on the agreements when a solution of the other kind, the "Multilateral Force," was conceived and pressed forward—the MLF scheme for a mixed-manned fleet of ships equipped with Polaris missiles jointly financed, owned, and controlled. The British didn't like this plan for a number of reasons, some of them purely technical, but our main objection arose from a lack of conviction that it would attain the ends that it set out to reach. And, I may say, our doubts were shared by a considerable number of other NATO countries. In fact, only eight of them agreed even to discuss the MLF proposal, and, after two years of discussion, only two, the United States and Germany, were ready to commit themselves to joining. At the same time the French, who had earlier been rather neutral and disinterested, came out positively against it. Almost everybody now agrees that the MLF will not command general support within the Alliance.

In the meantime, the British have put forward a proposal for a multilateral solution to the problems of sharing responsibility for nuclear strategy. We call it the Atlantic Nuclear Force, and we hope that it may prove to be more generally acceptable because it seems closer to meeting the basic political requirement. Briefly, the British government is offering to place the V-bomber force and, later on, the Polaris submarines under the joint control of an authority made up from all the participants in the force. The counterpart would be an equivalent contribution of American weapons to the force under the same control arrangements, and the third component would be a mixed-manned element in which the non-nuclear countries could take an active and tangible part. This third component might be made up of aircraft or surface ships armed with Polaris missiles, along the lines of the original MLF scheme. Included in the proposal is that there be a specific undertaking by the parties against the dissemination of nuclear weapons. Conceivably, the plan might prove to be one the French could one day accept. (I hope I'm not being too optimistic.) At any rate, the proposals are designed to leave the door open for France. A very great effort of imagination is going to be required of every member, especially the United States, if we are to find a way of reconciling America's quasi-monopoly of

Western nuclear power and a continued American veto on its use with the legitimate and irresistible pressure for shared responsibility and enhanced status for the Europeans. I believe the path lies in wide and far-reaching interdependence among NATO countries, including deeper and more consistent political consultation and a more intensive system of crisis management. It is not at that last, desperate moment of decision—to use or not to use nuclear weapons—that consultation among allies is important. Then, consultation is probably too late. Rather in time of peace and in the early stages of critical situations, must we consult. In the final analysis one man has to decide, and we all know that it will be the President of the United States. Our aim must be to see that his decision, when it is taken, shall be based, and known by all to be based, on a full understanding of the feelings and judgments of the Western world as a whole.

I think it will be clear from this outline I have drawn of the nature of British defense commitments that my country is faced with some difficult problems. Any solutions we find must take into account several hard facts. In the world as it is today, we can no longer think in terms of a completely independent British policy, whether in relation to our friends and allies or to the communist world and the uncommitted world. (This is at least partly true of all other countries, including the United States and the Soviet Union.) We have reached a quite conscious conclusion that our foreign-policy aims can be achieved most effectively through alliances and through all forms of co-operation with like-minded countries. This is why being a reliable ally is an important part of our self-interest. To be a reliable ally we have to have a soundly based home

economy. For a medium-sized industrial nation, vitally
dependent on imported raw materials and sources of energy,
this implies the ability to trade round the world with the
minimum of restrictions and on the best terms we can
get. So we have a basic interest in peace and order and
in the sanctity of agreements. This explains our support
of the United Nations, our deep concern for disarmament,
and our hope for an extension of the present détente
between East and West.

Frederick E. Nolting

Status and Prospects of the Western Alliance

MY CONVICTION that there is a major need for overhauling the structure of our alliances comes hard for me, for I am devoted to NATO, its principles, its proud history, and its dedicated servitors. I have spent many years of my life working for NATO, and I am not by nature or experience attracted to panaceas for the ever evolving problems of international relations. But I am not satisfied with the status quo of our Free World alliances, nor do I think that patchwork attempts to fix them up are going to prove successful.

You may be surprised if I work into the subject of international alliances by way of Viet Nam. Not only do I have a very deep and personal interest in that question, but Viet Nam also serves to illustrate a point I want to make. Recently the news appeared in the press that conversations were going on between the French and Soviet governments, on the one hand, and the British and Soviet governments, on the other, concerning negotiations for a settlement of the Vietnamese struggle. These conversations were reportedly taking place with the foreknowledge of the United States government, though to what extent they were approved by the government was not clear. At about the same time, the Secretary General of the United Nations, Mr. U Thant, was said to be pressing for negotiations. The impression given at that time—and it still persists—was that two of our principal allies, France and Britain (although the latter's position was obscure), together with the Soviet Union and the Secretary General of the United Nations, were, each from a different direction, putting the squeeze on the United States to "negotiate out" of our commitment in Viet Nam, as we had—disastrously, I think—in Laos in 1962. The Soviet Union was apparently cast in the role of "honest broker" in this deal—a role it had been supposed to play, but didn't, in the so-called settlement in Laos.

These recent developments in the Viet Nam problem reinforce my view that our alliances are inadequate in scope to meet present needs. Here we are confronted with the spectacle of a major split among leading NATO countries; total inaction of the part of SEATO (the responsible defense alliance in this case); an independent and apparently freewheeling intervention by the head of the United Nations (whose organization is itself paralyzed by the no-vote agreement); no apparent alignment of position with Australia and New Zealand under the ANZUS Treaty (although Australia, especially, has for years been actively involved in support of free Viet Nam); and no reported alignment of views under other United States bilateral treaties, notably with Japan, the Philippines, and Nationalist China, which are crucial to our position in the Pacific. And to further complicate the picture, we are told that the United States is sounding out Communist China, with whom we have no official dealings, to find out in "unofficial" talks between the United States and Chinese ambassadors in Warsaw what Peking's "real" position is on the Viet Nam question. If the internal situation in Viet Nam seems confused, I submit that the international situation surrounding it is a veritable basket of crabs. Under such circumstances, I ask myself, is it possible to solve, within the existing framework of NATO, problems of the most far-reaching importance to all free nations—such as the maintenance of an inviolable defense and deterrent; the reunification of Germany; East-West boundaries and contacts; the sharing of nuclear power; a sound position on disarmament, trade, and financial problems; and, fundamental to them all, basic agreement on the policies to be pursued on all continents and in all areas of our shrinking world?

Major developments in the Far East are imminent, I think, and cannot be long delayed. To pretend that these developments, whatever they may be, will not affect the future of the Western Alliance would be foolishly unrealistic. If there is one thing that experience has taught us, it is this: An alliance that lacks the will and unity to project and expand its influence is like a tree without water—it is doomed to die. I pray to God that this will not happen to NATO. If it does, communism will have won the major battle of our century.

And so it may not be too farfetched to approach the subject of Free World alliances (the strongest of which is NATO) via Saigon, Viet Nam. If you consider this a long way around, I invite your attention to the fact that today, in terms of time (the modern way of looking at space, which, incidentally, marks a very important evolution in our thinking), Saigon is ten times closer to Washington, D. C., than Williamsburg, Virginia, was to Philadelphia in 1776. But lest it be inferred that Viet Nam has been singled out as a special case of NATO non-solidarity because it is there that *our* ox is being gored, we should remember that NATO, as such, did nothing to help find solutions for the long and terrible problems France faced in Indo-China and later in Algeria. Nor do I recall NATO's helping the Dutch to find a solution in Indonesia or later in New Guinea, or helping the Belgians, more recently, in the Congo. These observations are made, not to downgrade NATO's accomplishments over the last fifteen years—for I truly believe that without NATO there would have been a major war over the issue of western Europe—but only to suggest that NATO's co-operation has been limited in scope—too limited, I think, to meet the requirements of today.

The other papers in this volume, which range from dis-cussions of defense policy to political consultation, seem to pay little attention to the fact that two of the NATO countries, Canada and the United States, flank the Pacific. The main focus is on Europe and the Atlantic, which, of course, is natural. But in reading the discussion of our German colleague, in particular, about the American con-tribution to European defense—what it has been and what it ought to be in tactical and in strategic forces—I wondered whether some of our European partners have ever faced the question of how they would fulfill their treaty commitments in the event of a Russian incursion across the one hundred mile strait into the State of Alaska. I do not raise this question as a serious defense problem, but I do raise it in an effort to take the blinders off some of our partners, and to suggest that sharing of defense responsibilities is a two-way street. For I am convinced that, in this shrinking world, an alliance must extend its united influence to ever expanding areas if it is to remain effectively united at the center. In this, though I do not pretend to understand him very well, I think I agree with President de Gaulle.

Can we expect NATO solidarity in the problem we face in Viet Nam today? I hope that we can. But in all honesty we must recognize that non-solidarity, or non-involvement, on the part of NATO has been the rule when the issues were not immediately central to the defense of the treaty area. I do not think this is good enough, imaginative enough, or even sound, in the interrelated world of today. And, I repeat, I say this not solely because it is the United States which is on the front line in Viet Nam.

Seldom, I think, has the need for straight thinking, imagination, sound judgment, and clear leadership been greater. It is commonplace, but true, to say that this necessity is forced upon us by the breakthroughs of science, which have resulted not only in thermonuclear armaments and intercontinental missiles, but also in media of mass education, instant and vivid communication, and travel into the remotest areas of the world and, shortly, into outer space. How do these obvious and oft repeated facts affect our thinking about international organizations? There have been very few significant changes in international organizations during the past ten years (aside from the growth in membership of the United Nations). Yet problems in the field of foreign relations are multiplying at an alarming rate; and few, if any, of the old problems are being solved, or even moved off dead center. In the field of collective action, it seems to me that institutional overlaps, institutional gaps, and institutional paralysis have so confused public opinion that there is danger of serious disillusionment and a reversion to isolationism and extreme nationalism. And to move in the direction of isolationism would, I think, be a stupid move; for it would be contrary to the logic of physical discovery and technology, which certainly tend to tie the world together. Instead of retreating to isolationism, should we not seriously tackle the problem of adapting international organizations to present requirements? This, obviously, is a large and difficult task. It would affect, I should think, all of the international organizations of which the United States is a member. It would affect NATO, and here special care would be required to assure that the delicate power equation, on which so much depends, is not upset.

You have read a great deal in this volume about the origins of NATO, its evolution and growth, and the various facets of its activities—military, political, social, and economic. Other contributors have given you a closer look at the difficulties which now beset it than I can, and a better understanding of the search for areas of common will and action which are essential for growth, but which are increasingly difficult to find. You have by now an appreciation of the changes in the will and drive of the Alliance, brought about by the détente with Soviet Russia, by the increased prosperity of western Europe, and by the divergent views held by the major members on fundamental questions.

You can feel the effect upon the Alliance of bitter internal disputes, such as those centering on Cyprus and the Portugese problem of Angola and Mozambique. You have seen the evolution of conditions and attitudes which have diminished the effectiveness of the Alliance from what it was fifteen, ten, or even five years ago. You can sense the frustrations arising from the fruitless search for an acceptable formula for the sharing of nuclear power, and the political currents set in motion by the apparent failure of the MLF, a halfway house that nobody seems anxious to buy or even to rent. And yet it is a fact, I think, that no member country wishes to abandon NATO, and none wants it to fail. It has been too valuable a thing in this world. It can continue to be so, and it can become even more of an influence for good provided we find the proper areas and means for its growth and adaptation to new conditions.

The physical power of NATO was built, as you know, in direct response to the menace of Soviet Russia's armed strength and expansionist policy. There is no doubt, anywhere in the Alliance, that the armed strength of the U.S.S.R. has continued to grow and is now at a very high level. In a recent speech discussing NATO's defense requirements in relation to the capabilities of the Soviet bloc's armed forces, General Lemnitzer said:

To sustain the level of effort needed, there must be continuing recognition of the very real urgency of the requirement facing us. Naturally, political negotiations to reduce East-West tensions must be unceasing. The prospects for the success of our negotiations, however, rest to an important degree on our military strength. Any apparent signs that the Soviet Bloc might be softening its attitude would be encouraging. But there can be no grounds for relaxing our *military* effort—which is clearly and exclusively aimed at our collective defense—so long as the Soviet Bloc nations continue to maintain what all national intelligence agencies and NATO intelligence staffs agree to be very substantial, well trained and powerfully armed and equipped military forces.

.   .   .   .

Military planning has only one valid basis—the capabilities which the potential enemy is known to possess. It cannot rely on what it is assumed that the opponent *intends* to do.

This, to my mind, is sound military advice; it is also elementary prudence and common sense. SACEUR's comments, properly, leave unanswered the question of Soviet intentions. To what extent has the expansionist drive of the Soviet Union been ameliorated? It is basically on this question, I think, that opinions differ and policies diverge. It does not seem to me that the evidence today warrants any complacency on this subject on the part of any free country. On the contrary, no matter what changes we may detect or anticipate in Soviet tactics, NATO's deterrent strength will continue to be essential for the freedom of western Europe until the capabilities of the communist armed forces to commit aggression are lessened or removed. It is a somber fact that there has been no real advance in the negotiations on disarmament in Geneva, nor in the attempts to devise a safe and effective limitation or inspection of armaments and armed forces in Central Europe.

To revert to the Far East—as you see, I am obsessed by the interrelationship of these matters—we find a pertinent example in Laos in 1962. As you recall, SEATO was split on how to counter increasing communist advances in Laos. The United States finally went along with the views of Britain and France, and a conference was called at Geneva to work out a peaceful settlement. As we became more deeply involved in hard bargaining with the communist side (including Russia, China, and North Viet Nam), it became increasingly clear that we were risking more and more on the good faith of those communist countries. We were told by certain officials in the Department of State that we could rely on the Russians to "police" the Chinese and North Vietnamese—to see to it that they did not violate the agreements. The treaty was finally signed, without adequate safeguards or an enforcement mechanism, and the United States withdrew its support from the elements in Laos which had been actively resisting communist advances. But the North Vietnamese and Pathet Lao, backed by the Chinese, immediately used the agreements as a screen for further advances, both in Laos and in South Viet Nam, and even into Thailand. They used the agreements to secure their hold on the routes into Viet Nam— the very routes we are now trying to interdict by U. S. Air Force bombing. Whether or not the Russians tried to "police" them I do not know. But I do know the net result. We were *had*.

If, as is sometimes claimed, the Geneva agreements on Laos widened the gap between Peking and Moscow, this has not been evident in recent events in Viet Nam. I do not know the inside story—and I recognize that this is a tricky business—but it seems to me that recent events in Viet Nam have shown that China and Russia, in a showdown with the United States, will close ranks. Yet this is no reason, I am sure you will agree, to shrink from the call of duty and national interest in sustaining the independence of South Viet Nam. For regardless of past mistakes and present splits, our national interests compel us to see to it that South Viet Nam retains its independence.

History has assigned to our country in this century the role of leader in defending and promoting an expanding philosophy of life and government. To fulfill that role is both difficult and hazardous. We could make it easier,

I think, by giving a clearer lead to those who share our principles.

What are those principles? They derive, I think, mainly, but not exclusively, from two sources: the philosophy of ancient Greece and the Judeo-Christian ethic. From Socrates, Plato, and Aristotle came the idea that man is capable, through reason, of making sound judgments; and from this evolved the concept and practice of democracy and self-government. From Christ came the concepts of compassion, love, and service; and from these evolved the ideal that one had a responsibility to help other people, both within and without one's own country. However short we and other like-minded nations fall of fulfilling these ideals, they remain, I think, the true basis of our influence in the world. The founding fathers of NATO based their hopes for a continuing and deepening alliance upon these fundamental attitudes. I should like to propose that we give them more serious attention, more systematic expression, and more universal application as a basis for a rejuvenated and expanded alliance of free peoples.

Over the years, the cement of fear has somehow lost much of its effectiveness in NATO. How do we go about building an alliance with more permanent cement—the cement of a compelling common philosophy? The challenge is great; the complications and obstacles are enormous. But let us not hesitate to think big. Others have thought big. Consider what the Soviet Union has accomplished in less than fifty years by a single-minded exploitation of a basic and revolutionary idea, however costly that idea has been in terms of human values. Did anyone think, forty years ago, that the Soviet Union would become the world power that it is today? And Communist China, what are her prospects? Perhaps you will remember that some ten years ago there was the widely held belief—

which turned out to be based on the sheerest wishful
thinking—that Mao Tse-tung would never be able to organize the "unorganizable" Chinese people, or regiment
six hundred million of them to consolidate his revolution.
Today the whole of Southeast Asia stands in the shadow
of Chinese power, and the continent of Africa is being
systematically penetrated. I do not say these things to
eulogize communist regimes. I despise communist regimes
on moral grounds. But we must face that fact that they
have been effective. And they have been effective mainly,
I think, because they have exploited a single motivating
idea continuously and consistently. The people of the Free
World have a much better idea. The philosophy of life
and of government shared by NATO nations and many
others is worth preserving, improving, and extending for
the benefit of mankind. How can we organize ourselves to
project it more effectively?

Certainly, prudence as well as imagination is necessary.
We cannot afford to abandon or weaken the alliances we
have while seeking to devise better and more effective ones.
But I should like to indicate the direction in which perhaps we should be thinking and planning.

First, it seems to me that *regional* organizations for defense purposes are not adequate to meet today's requirements. There are no geographic limits to communist subversion. Regional collective-security arrangements are too
limited, I believe, to meet the present threat.

Second, given the nuclear stalemate, a greater proportion of the attention, ingenuity, and resources of free nations should be shifted from static defense planning to active projection of our ideas and principles. I do not mean
for one moment that our physical defenses should be allowed to fall behind the enemy's capabilities. Nor do I
mean to imply that our form of government is suitable for

all peoples. But I do think that the people of the Free World have been too long on the defensive, both in their thinking and in their planning. Our collective-defense alliances, in particular, need reorganizing and redirection to remedy this deficiency.

If, then, geographically limited alliances and present concepts of defense are not suited to today's form of attack—political undermining, aggressive subversion, and communist-inspired "wars of liberation"—what is the most effective way, assuming we have the common sense to tackle the problem collectively? I would suggest that consideration be given by a group of like-minded states, in whatever continents they may be found, to banding together on the basis of certain criteria governing both their internal and external policies. Such criteria might include an agreed level of public education; a demonstrated record of governmental stability and public law, and an effective code of justice; evidence of sound public financial policy; an agreed-upon degree of participation in and contribution to joint measures to combat subversion, both within member states and elsewhere; and a commitment to contributing to the development of countries not yet ready for membership but aspiring to it.

The organization of such a group, comprising countries in many parts of the world, would not be a simple thing, but it would have enormous advantages. It would not necessarily cut across or weaken existing regional defense arrangements, but it would provide a larger framework into which certain Free World defense responsibilities could eventually be fitted. Above all, I think it would form a pole of attraction for emerging nations by providing a center for clear and consistent projection of the basic values of free societies.

If this seems far out, I ask you to consider that there is no such center at present. The United Nations does not provide it, I am sorry to say. NATO, as valuable as it has been and is today, needs to raise its sights and to view the world entire. Its failure to do so is, I think, the root cause of the dissentions within it today. The basic principles on which the Western Alliance rests—liberty, justice, and human advancement—have millions of adherents in all parts of the world, including those outside the confines of the North Atlantic Treaty areas. Let us consider ways to give these people a place to go where there is encouragement in the realization of those ideals and where free men together can take the offensive. I have faith that the difficulties now besetting our Free World alliances can be transcended if we are bold enough to plan ahead while holding to the good already accomplished through collective will and action.

In conclusion, I should attempt to pull together and summarize these thoughts on the status and prospects of the Western Alliance and its place in the world. I should confess that I tried very hard to write a more traditional paper on NATO—one that would be more analytical and specific, dealing with the Alliance as it is and perhaps suggesting some ways to improve it. Instead, I have reached the conclusion that the Western Alliance (as best exemplified in NATO, with its multiplicity of organs) is, or should be, approaching a period of transition. That transition, I suggest, should transform it by stages from a limited, geographically defined defense alliance to a much broader, world-wide organization of like-minded states, qualified for membership by their adherence to certain standards of national and international behavior. Such an organization would be open-ended and would constitute, I would hope,

a pole of attraction for developing nations in all parts of
the world. It should not bear the label "Western." It
should, however, have conspicuously in its charter the
word "responsible." It should be bound by treaty not only
to defend, but also to promote, agreed-upon principles of
human liberty and government by consent. It should have,
as a major instrument, a collective-defense organization,
including an integrated military staff and as much integration of forces as possible. Such forces should be available
for, among other things, use in dealing with communist-
sponsored "wars of liberation."

During the long and difficult period required to form
such an organization (in which, I would hope, the members
of NATO, drawing on their experience, would play a leading part), existing collective-defense arrangements should,
of course, be maintained, and, if possible, strengthened—
NATO especially. But, as I have indicated, I do not believe
that the basic factors now impeding NATO's progress are
likely to be solved within its existing framework. Over the
last decade, many things have changed in the world,
making necessary, I believe, corollary changes in international organization and co-operation. The growth and importance of world trade, the shifts in economic and power
relationships, the shrinking of our planet in terms of dis-
tance and communications, and the shift in communist
tactics resulting from the two-way nuclear deterrent—to
mention only a few— impel us all, I think, to consider new
forms for organized co-operation among free nations. I
hope our country, with its great power and manifold responsibilities and its proven record of international co-
operation, will again take the lead in thinking through these
complex problems.

Edgar S. Furniss, Jr.

A Personal Evaluation of the Western Alliance

DESIGNED to meet a crisis, the Western Alliance has, since its inception, been a part of that crisis. An examination of Alliance problems in isolation would only becloud even further the relationships among the members and complicate immeasurably the task of evaluating national policies. Rather must the Alliance be viewed in the context of the East-West antagonisms that produced it. Is a crisis which lasts almost twenty years to be regarded as a crisis at all? Has it not by this time become, for better or for worse, almost a way of life? Proposals to remove or at least to lessen difficulties among the members take on one aspect if the goal is maintenance or strengthening of the Alliance as an international system. The same proposals appear in a different light if the objective is to advance solutions to East-West tensions which threaten the entire world community with destruction. And the difference is by no means simply that of the short (practical) range and the long (visionary) range.

Not surprisingly, the distinguished contributors to this volume are in general agreement on a number of points. That the formation of the Alliance was indispensable to keeping western Europe free from Soviet communist control, they do not doubt. That NATO, through its vicissitudes, has been the key factor in maintaining the security of its members, they also affirm. They appear also to concur in the post-1960 assessment that the power position of western Europe vis-à-vis the East was far better than had previously been adjudged.

While such a consensus and the evidence on which it is based provide sources of pride in past action and hope for future policy, is not the record just a bit more complicated than it sometimes is made to appear? By the time the North Atlantic Treaty was signed (April, 1949), to say nothing of the time the Organization itself began to emerge (December, 1950), the nature of American intent was already apparent and had produced some significant effects. As early as March, 1947, the United States under the Truman Doctrine had plainly indicated its willingness to assume military responsibilities no longer capable of being discharged by weakened, overcommitted allies. While immediately ensuing policy focused on strengthening the Greek and Turkish governments, the Doctrine was potentially of general applicability. In the era of American atomic monopoly, the warning to would-be aggressors was an obvious and most serious one.

In western Europe, analogous actions were being taken, two of which were pivotal. American occupation policy in Germany was clearly turning from punishment to rehabilitation, on the road to partnership. With the acquiescence of the impoverished British and against the vehement opposition of the ineffectual French, the United States took steps to promote the political and economic viability of that portion of the erstwhile enemy not under Russian control. Unmistakable Soviet intent to thwart Four-Power administration and to convert its occupation zone into a communist satellite was answered by the equally clear intent of the United States to build a "situation of strength" on the western side of the confrontation line.

Simultaneously, the United States was embarking on what became a multibillion dollar program to revive the economies of other western European countries, as well as that of occupied West Germany. The political implications of American aid were plain, particularly in France and Italy. Participation by Communists and their relatives in executive coalitions was neither desirable nor necessary. Anticommunist, anti-Soviet governments, on the other hand, could count on the help of the United States in rebuilding their countries, with all the vote-getting prestige entailed therein. Russian and Eastern satellite withdrawal from the conference to implement General Marshall's proposal made possible the definitive blending of economics and politics. In sum, the *Alliance* had already emerged when the *Treaty* was signed. Like most treaties, the North Atlantic Pact publicized and made official the pre-existing relationship. It also added the most logical ingredient, the one foreshadowed by the Brussels Pact as well as the Truman Doctrine. By the military guarantee entwined in the Treaty's provisions, the United States put the Eastern antagonist on notice that it was prepared to act if necessary to protect its investment—the Alliance it had fostered. Moreover, the American response to Russian pressures on West Berlin demonstrated that the United States had no intention of abandoning any segment of the Alliance, however exposed it might be, and was prepared in its defense to exercise as diversified a statecraft as might be required.

As with the Treaty, so with the Organization, the place ultimately assigned to it by history may be rather different from that envisioned by the founding fathers or by subsequent official spokesmen. Only when Soviet archives become available to Western scholars (a happy day) will we be able to say with certainty. In the meantime, some speculations seem justified. Quite clearly, the Organization served the important purpose of making the American guarantee believable to various onlookers: the Russians, the west Europeans (particularly the West Germans), and the American people. Therefore, the whirling of gears, while contributing to the building and positioning of allied military power, also had significance as testimony to the fact that an Organization did indeed exist, that because it was directed by Americans, it was closely fitted to United States plans for the employment of the full panoply of American weaponry. As successor to the Brussels Pact, the Organization was also concrete evidence that the European countries remained determined to protect one another, as well as to accept protection from their transatlantic ally. This principle of self-help was particularly important in the United States, where it was established as an indispensable prerequisite to American material assistance. For the first years after the Treaty was signed, military aid, of course, provided the foundation for whatever indigenous strength there was in Europe. The American-led Organization thus provided a system for relating United States power outside Europe to United States power in Europe and to United States power transferred to European hands.

As is well known, the allied commitment to the principle of self-help was never matched by concrete performance judged satisfactory by American political and military leaders. A rationale for continued American leadership in the Organization was thereby provided at the same time that American standards of measurement were used as justifications for continuing the process of re-creating a strong Germany. Thus, NATO performed two other, internal functions, both related to the former enemy. Ultimately, the Organization assumed supervisory responsibility for the new German military establishment, thereby promoting and at the same time inhibiting the emergence of a distinct western European system in which Germany would take its place beside France and, possibly, Great Britain as a leading figure. The substitution of the wildly misnamed Western European Union for the European Defense Community was far more than a shift in nomenclature. The difference in structure reflects the difference in two concepts of *European* organization and of its relationship to the United States.

Without great exaggeration, it may be said that a most important purpose of the North Atlantic Treaty Organization in the first decade of NATO's existence was organization.

Contributors to this volume also join in identifying three related problems which now beset the Alliance. One stems from the belief on the part of many groups in many European countries that the possibility of an armed attack from the Soviet Union has become remote. A second arises from the behavior of General-President Charles de Gaulle, and the interpretations placed thereon by various allies. Finally, nuclear technology has produced allied demands for sharing in decisions concerning nuclear strategy and has made all too real the specter of accelerating nuclear-weapons proliferation.

The range of solutions advanced with regard to all three problems can best be analyzed in terms of differing conceptions which exist of the contemporary nature and purposes of the Western Alliance. Superficially, it is ironic that perceptions of a diminished Soviet threat should constitute one of the problems. Isn't it a good thing that most people in most countries share a greater sense of security? Not necessarily. There is dispute over the degree of increased security. There are differences in predictions concerning future trends. There are variations in the national sources of these perceptions, in their intensity, in their effect on policy prescriptions. Finally, differences in identified causes produce arguments over problematic consequences. Because events rudely intrude to upset their calculations, it is not surprising that successive national leaders, and even the same ones, have presented a variety of combinations of interpretations concerning the Russian menace. Since the value and future of the Alliance are dependent on these views, re-creation of a multinational consensus becomes virtually impossible if Soviet policy does not help by reverting to simplified patterns of the immediate postwar period or Alliance leadership does not find new ways of buying or coercing acquiescence to one, sanctioned judgment. The first is highly unlikely. The impact of external and internal events on Soviet leadership has manifestly changed Russian policy, not least toward western Europe. Coincidentally, Western analysts now know or think they know so much about factors influencing

Soviet statecraft that they are no longer content with a single value, goal, technique model for explanation and prediction.

Purchased or coerced acquiescence is likewise difficult to envisage because structural relations within the Alliance have profoundly altered since 1949. It has previously been suggested that the original concept was that of the great (American) giant protecting the frail (European) pygmies. In this relationship, consensus concerning the Soviet threat hardly needed to be sought. The original formulation, however, was regarded as temporary, pending the uniting of western Europe with American help and inspiration, so that members of the Alliance could help themselves more and depend on their protector less. A Continental combination would, in other words, assume greater responsibilities; but without some agreement on the nature of the threat, a judgment could hardly be reached on whether responsive action was responsible or irresponsible.

Thus the essence of the second concept of the Alliance was superiority of the larger, NATO system over the smaller, European system. Military defense was assumed to have first priority, and, as monopolist of the major deterrent force, the United States would continue to delineate defense requirements. While encouraged to proceed with integrative efforts in the economic field and to look forward to political unity, the European system was not to develop its own military organization. Separation of roles was paralleled by assignment of permissible weaponry within the all-inclusive institution of the Alliance.

At this point, the "French problem" emerges as an attack on the idea that the Alliance is composed of a superior and a subordinate system, with agreed-upon divisions of power and responsibility and equally acceptable limits on development. De Gaulle poses questions which are neither new nor confined to France. What is original is the style and persistence in which they are stated and restated, and the lengths to which the autocratic leader appears willing to go to obtain acceptable answers from the allies. Concerning the nature of the Soviet threat, the president of France, in effect, asks two questions. What does it profit NATO to keep the Soviet Union at bay in Europe while allowing the forces of international communism, their satraps, and their dupes, successfully to eliminate Western interests and influences in other parts of the world? If it be admitted that the first is an important question, then the second is all the more difficult to shrug off: Who is to be regarded as the legitimate interpreter of any Soviet threat anywhere and, therefore, of the appropriate responses to be made by the Alliance— its transatlantic initiator or the nations of Europe most immediately affected?

These questions can only artificially be separated from others concerning nuclear technology which have also been raised by Gaullist France. If nuclear weaponry is the ultimate arbiter, why should one member of the Alliance be able to engage the others outside the NATO area in the consequences of its actions? Within the Western Alliance itself, why should the United States be permitted to preserve a quasi-monopoly on the production of nuclear weapons systems, when it has long since lost this position to its primary, global antagonist and now apparently is losing it to the second pillar of international communism as well?

In place of the present relationship, De Gaulle suggests an alliance responsible for framing (but in all probability not implementing) Western policy, particularly nuclear policy, all over the world. In organizational terms, that alliance would, like the aforementioned concept, embrace two major parts—the United States and a "European Europe." The latter, however, would, if De Gaulle had his way, be raised to a position of approximate equality with the United States as regards policy formation, though not in military power or in responsibility for policy implementation. The organization of this European Europe would be multinational and comprehensive, rather than supranational and non-military. It would command a nuclear arsenal appropriate to its needs, produced by individual and collective efforts of its members and supplemented, if necessary, by assistance from a belatedly enlightened, transatlantic ally. As might be expected from this Gaullist formulation, the linchpins holding the Alliance together would be the United States and France. American power would remain in Europe until and unless Americans decided to withdraw (an event sometimes forecast) or an augmented European deterrent capacity made their more than token presence happily unnecessary. Reciprocally, France would participate with the United States in framing global Alliance strategy, and in possible partnership with Great Britain, provided the British foreswore vain pretensions to an Anglo-American partnership and unequivocally cast their lot with Europe.

De Gaulle has demonstrated his intention of going very far in unilateral policy to attain his objective. He appears to favor the maintenance of some kind of Alliance but with such a dismantling of the Organization that, as the present writer has frequently commented, the O would be removed from NATO. European integration is to be equivalently limited, also to preserve the autonomy of national decision. Of late, less has been said about common Alliance policy outside the NATO area; but more oracular pronouncements have been made concerning the desirable direction for settlement of outstanding issues in Europe, including as one ingredient an "inspirational" definition of Europe itself. Whether Gaullists see a western European nuclear capacity as having any relevance to the settlement of issues on the Continent is not clear. Equally uncertain is whether such a capacity would entail development of conventional arms levels and call for a reassignment of national responsibilities within the spectrum of deterrence and defense.

Before one can attempt to categorize the range of solutions to the problems of the Western Alliance, particular mention must be made of one American effort, discussed by many of the contributors to this volume. As a response to presumed European restiveness over exclusion from nuclear strategy, the nuisances perpetrated by De Gaulle, and the quarrels over the contemporary seriousness of the Soviet threat, United States leadership polished a set of ideas until they shone forth as the Multilateral Nuclear Force. The concept of the Alliance on which the MLF rested might be characterized as the product of idealism and desperation. The ideal goal postulated for American statecraft was a united Europe no longer conceived of as an inferior system in the all-important matter of defense. For lack of a directed verdict on military means and responsibilities, policy would reflect a continuing consensus on Alliance requirements and Continental contributions. The recurrent nerve-jangling dissonance produced by the breakdown of American authority within the Alliance and military supremacy outside it would be replaced by a reasoned harmony of the two spheres.

The desperation could be seen in the hope of its advocates that the MLF would somehow provide a "solution" to the advance (on-rush) of nuclear-weapons proliferation. Cautious optimism was expressed that ultimately a "European authority" would emerge, to which responsibility could be assigned for managing any Continental dimension of over-all Alliance nuclear power. In the meantime, the MLF constituted a positive response to presumed European "demands" for "sharing" in formulating and executing allied statecraft. Present prospects and future possibilities supposedly would cause non-nuclear allies to remain so, and nuclear allies to abandon their national efforts.

Few words of praise can be found in this volume for the MLF. And no wonder. Despite concentrated salesmanship (abroad) by its American proponents, it created more apprehension than it allayed. The argument could not long be sustained that the device added to Western military power. On the political level, the MLF was quickly revealed as incapable of producing an Alliance united by a freely given consensus on ends and means and resting on interlocking European and American systems. For some in Europe, MLF was a response to a demand they had not made; they were far more trusting of American direction of nuclear statecraft than of potential European participants. For others, the day of a politically integrated Europe was still far off, and the American proposal seemed either to postpone it still further or to make it undesirable altogether.

As national positions clarified, the MLF emerged as primarily a device to help contemporary West German leadership in extending the already strong German-American suballiance. With Gaullist France a vitriolic antagonist of the whole idea, the MLF could hardly masquerade

as a solution to the problem of *existing* nuclear prolifiera-
tion; whether it would notably delay or advance the ad-
vent of German national nuclear capability was a moot
question. Great Britain, pressed hard for a constructive
suggestion, came up with what it called an Allied Nuclear Force, couched, deliberately or not, in such vague
terms as to suggest that the real purpose was to bury the
whole issue under a thick layer of obfuscatory dust. Since
no united Europe was in the immediate offing and Britain
had no intention of joining if there had been one, the ANF,
if taken seriously, would imply a system far closer to the
multinational one sought by De Gaulle than to the integrated force proposed by Americans.

The deep-freezing of the Multilateral Nuclear Force in
late 1964 (possibly only until the German, French, [and
British?] elections have been held) appears to some European statesmen to illustrate a deliberate softening of American leadership within the Western Alliance. Allied affairs
are allowed to drift, despite the existence of the Organization, to the lowest level of the most reluctant. While the
United States tangles itself more thoroughly in Viet Nam
(the soothing word is "escalation") and sends the marines to
arbitrate the political affairs of the Dominican Republic
(operation "preventive anti-Castroism"), General-President
de Gaulle goes merrily about his business of pulling the
Organization apart. In 1969, the Treaty can be denounced,
on one year's notice (Article 13). Will there then be anything left worth denouncing?

Since 1959, collective consultation to review the Treaty
has been possible on the initiative of any member (Article
12). The types of changes which might be advanced in any
such review are forecast by the contributors to this volume.

They may be categorized under four headings: Make the structure of the Alliance stronger, with or without *Gaullist* France. Take steps to unite further the European side of the Alliance. While seeking to strengthen the Alliance, devote concentrated efforts to adding something new in Western organization. Finally, leave things—at least major things—alone. Each type of suggestion reflects expectations concerning the evolution of the international environment in general, and of allied interrelationships in particular. Thus, value judgments are entailed concerning the proper place of the Alliance in future Western statecraft.

NATO was designed to concert allied military policy in western Europe under American guidance, not to integrate total allied military policy, not to concert non-military policy, except in direct relation to defensive power, not to convert an Alliance into a regional security system. Now there are some who would enlarge the scope of the Organization to embrace one or more of the areas originally excluded. Previous proposals, of which there have been many, have produced little result, with the noteworthy exception of fuller and franker *discussion*. That more was not done is clearly the responsibility of the United States. Even now many steps could be taken if the United States were prepared to make the requisite sacrifices and lead an Alliance without or, if need be, against De Gaulle. Command structures could be reorganized, their headquarters shifted; economic, social, and cultural agencies added. The Secretary-General and the Secretariat could be endowed with more authority and with an enlarged and more diversified staff to exercise it. Procedures could be established to handle disputes among members first or exclusively within the confines of the Organization, thereby endowing it with collective-security features akin to those of the Organization of American States. Persistent, publicized efforts could be made to hammer out in Organization meetings ingredients of a NATO policy on non-military matters in non-NATO areas.

All these things *could* be done, but the same factors inhibiting American statesmen are well recognized by other leaders. No matter how much obeisance is made to it, an Atlantic Community does not exist. Structural changes in the Organization might, in time, produce such a community; but potential members still perceive positive advantages in both the flexibility of, and limitation on, their commitments. Many of the allies have not been convinced that an alignment on policy on non-military issues and on issues concerning the non-NATO area is desirable. Desirable or not, divergences among the allies cause many to doubt whether any durable agreement could be reached, if attempted.

United States unilateral decisions to take forceful, unilateral action in Viet Nam and in the Dominican Republic illustrate both points. Once again, the leader of the Alliance has shown that, when confronted with certain types of crisis, it will act first and inform afterward, or inform with no effort to consult. The attitudes of the Western allies demonstrate that, if an Alliance position had been sought before American action was taken, delays would have occurred, and any emergent consensus would have been weak and, quite probably, ephemeral. One contributor to this book has pointed out that several members of the Western Alliance do not wish to assume the responsibility implied in a search for predecisional agreement on the entire range of questions of primary concern only to the larger states. Consciousness of limited power produces a desire for limited participation in the totality of Western statecraft.

The idea that a regrouping of non-communist nations should take place has the charm of the unexpected and the academic attraction of the superficially implausible. The rationale is all too evident. Whatever its successes in Europe, the Alliance has not been able to prevent the West from suffering spectacular reverses elsewhere; and Communist China's growing, independent power threatens still more to come. None of the Western nations, not even the United States, wishes to stand alone in Africa and Asia as the guardian of Western interests. Yet existing international organizations—the universal UN, the regional SEATO and CENTO, least of all NATO—have neither alleviated the causes of conflict nor successfully pooled power to frustrate aggressors.

Whether any "Friends of Liberty" group could effect a cure is problematic. Surely it has not been a paucity of organization which has prevented the West from dealing swiftly and effectively with threats to long-established and recent interests. Rather are diminished relative strength and weakened will writ large on the postwar record. Most Western nations have not sought to recapture or hold their pre-1939 positions. Sporadic moves to do so have revealed that close allies do not share the values implicit in such undertakings and, furthermore, that stability cannot for the most part be bought at reasonable military—or economic, or social, or political—rates. All the great powers, including most particularly the United States and the Soviet Union, share the same declining ability to manipulate the international environment to their purposes. To put the point in a different way, the era of frozen, hierarchic blocs has gone; the tide runs strongly toward flexibility and occasional interpenetration.

One new grouping (or a dozen) could hardly turn back the clock. If only the few mature Western democracies were included, it would resemble an exclusive White Man's Club, manning the eroded bastions of imperial privilege. If others were induced to join, all the contemporary defects of limited commitment and ideological reversal following governmental change would be repeated.

While all and sundry accept the proposition that much remains to be done to develop the European side of the Alliance, a disturbing cacophony arises as soon as discussions turn to the meaning of "develop" and of "Europe." Proponents of European "unity" hope that Gaullism will prove to be a passing aberration and that post-Gaullist France will rejoin the march toward federation. Certainly, the Fifth Republic has followed an intractable, unilateral, and somewhat puzzling line, which a future government might not pursue, if only because it lacked the necessary authoritarian direction. Previous pages, however, have suggested that the present road block (or ambush) is built on issues of means, members, and interests not easily removed by a change in French leadership.

Even if one grants that western European unity is desirable, the proper means to that end remain in dispute. Broadening the scope of existing communities would be one method, illustrated by the agreement to merge the European Commissions. Increasingly, national economic policies would be subordinated to community determination, while political institutions grew to maturity in the shelter of functional integration. There are these, however, who would reverse the order of economic and political unification in the belief that existing communities may prove to be inadequate or inappropriate integrators. The Council of Europe and Defense and Political Community drafts did not produce unity in those spheres, and now comes De Gaulle to renew the argument that broadened co-operation, but among governments, is necessary to avoid appropriation of Continental statecraft by economic "technocrats." The Gaullist, glacial approach to unity was embodied in the Fouchet Plan, rejected by France's partners, and publicized in the all but meaningless Franco-German Treaty.

Cutting through the miasma left by protracted, philosophical, abstract, and technical discussions over how to unify, one comes to the more fundamental questions of whom to unify and why to unify. Even its proponents gloomily acknowledge that unification cannot succeed without France. If France's policy remains that of co-operation among nations, why insist on more? Whether unification can proceed with Great Britain or without Great Britain is unknown. If Great Britain will only enter a Europe of international co-operation, why insist on more? Although the Common Market and Coal-Steel communities have made rapid progress—the former under the goading of Gaullist France, be it noted—the ultimate social orientation of both communities remains in doubt. If the subterranean struggle over social policy is won at the sacrifice of such interests as labor and the consumer, why unify? The desires of Western allies outside the Continental bloc are quite clearly for an outward looking, not introspective and parochial system and for one which makes attainment of a consensus on defense matters easier than in the past.

It is largely a matter of faith, not of fact, that a united Europe possessing these agreeable characteristics will emerge. If the record to date of community orientation, national action, and subnational group aspirations justifies doubts as to whether the mystique is justified, why rush to unify?

Why not, in short, wait and watch the emergence of "Europe," keeping open for the time being the myriad options between limited international co-operation and supranational political unification. Who speaks for Europe and what Europe speaks for are still problematical. Who speaks for the Western Alliance and what the Alliance speaks for are, it has been suggested, equally a matter of guesswork. Not merely inertia or astigmatism lie behind the notion that no dramatic, all-embracing steps are urgently required. At least for the United States, "dynamic do-nothingism" may be the best as well as the most prudent course. Perhaps we need to do more hard thinking about the probable direction of events and, therefore, about the goals and purposes of organization. When one looks ahead, it is difficult to resist the conclusion that powerful forces are propelling Western nations toward a complex layering of their international relationships. No one organization, indeed no grouping of organizations, can encompass all those relationships; the spectrum of interests and objectives defined by the foreign policies of the Western allies is too wide, the divisions between their domestic economies, social structures, and political systems too deep.

While preaching the gospel of unity, leaders of the Western Alliance have frequently acted in a different fashion. The United States has urged organization and unity for others; at the same time, it maintains a network of bilateral relations within the Alliance, as well as outside. Great Britain's problem of "to join or not to join" Europe lies in the extreme difficulty, bluntly pointed out by De Gaulle, of reconciling membership in a tightly organized, discriminatory Europe with interests and commitments elsewhere in the world. What wonder that authoritarian France should claim the same right to varying relations with different nations on different matters. Even West Germany, ostensibly the most integrationist of the larger allies, has made it abundantly clear that arrangements for European unity should not exclude close co-operation with Great Britain or weaken in any way its special ties to the United States. Since they have not been willing to hand over the same function to NATO, potential members observing the allies are hardly likely to make a future "Europe" exclusive arbiter of their policies in the area. Gaullist Franch has been able to call so many of the tunes because others have attached restrictions to European unity not simply because they are reluctant to proceed without France or have expected integration inexorably to occur with the participation of a post-Gaullist France.

It is a platitude frequently forgotten that the purpose of organization is not merely organization. Nor is it more and gaudier organizations, mysteriously produced by parturition. The justification for any organization can only be its contributions toward the solution of pre-existing, not self-created, problems. To protect a defenseless Europe through an American guarantee, the North Atlantic Treaty was signed. To give substance to that guarantee and to apportion responsibility for the defense of all, the North Atlantic Treaty Organization came into being. There was no expectation that Treaty or Organization would remove the situations producing the perceived threat, although they would serve as indispensable prerequisites to their removal. If hopes were entertained that NATO would be an instrument of "liberation," they were dispelled by allied reactions to the East German riots and the Hungarian rebellion. It was not anticipated that either Treaty or Organization would assist materially in resolving the inevitable difficulties among the allies arising from the revival of economic strength and political stability. Neither helped resolve the Saar question or Britain's search for accommodation with the Common Market. As it turned out, NATO was also powerless to prevent or settle political disputes among the members, whatever may have been the optimistic forecasts at one time or another. The Iceland fisheries embroglio may have had elements of the *opera bouffe*, but Suez shattered the Alliance temporarily, and Cyprus threatened to cause open war between two NATO members.

Most serious of all its limitations is that on East-West issues. If some form of legerdemain swept suddenly away all the obstacles to a greatly strengthened NATO and to a thoroughly integrated "Europe," would the prospect for East-West settlements on the Continent be improved? Once again, it is hard to resist, for all it is Gaullist, the logic of the proposition that shifting, complex patterns of cooperation resting on national foundations offer the best, if not the only hope that the nuclear confrontation of powerful antagonists in the heart of Europe may gradually be ended or at least made less dangerous. History's verdict should not be that the Western Alliance, becoming vitally dependent for its continued existence on high European tensions, organized its way toward catastrophe.

Notes on the Contributors

HORST BLOMEYER-BARTENSTEIN studied law and political science at the University of Munich and holds a Doctor's degree in law from this institution. He has taught simultaneously at the Institute for International Law and the Academy for Political Science. After entering the foreign service of the German Federal Republic, he was first assigned to the United States in 1958 when he came to the German Consulate General in San Francisco. In 1960, he became first secretary of the German Embassy in Washington, and in 1963 was appointed counselor, in which capacity he has specialized in politico-military affairs.

JENS M. BOYESEN was active in the Norwegian resistance during the German occupation of Norway in the years 1940-45. He completed his degree in law in 1947 and served as an assistant judge in the following year. In 1949, he entered the Norwegian foreign service, and, from 1951 to 1954, he held the position of undersecretary in the Ministry of Foreign Affairs. After serving in the Ministry of Defense during 1954 and 1955, he was appointed Norwegian ambassador to NATO and to the Organization for European Economic Co-operation, a post he held until 1963. In 1964, he accepted reappointment to his former position as undersecretary in the Ministry of Foreign Affairs.

EDGAR S. FURNISS, JR., is professor of political science and director of the Social Science Program of the Mershon Center for Education in National Security of the Ohio State University. He has studied at Yale University and the University of California at Berkeley, has held positions with the National Institute of Public Affairs and the Office of American Republic Affairs of the United States Department of State, and has taught at Yale, Princeton, Columbia, Pennsylvania, and Johns Hopkins universities, and at the Army, Navy, and Air war colleges. He is the author of *American Foreign Policy* (with Richard C. Snyder); *American Military Policy; France, Troubled Ally;* and *De Gaulle and the French Army.*

RICHARD GOOLD-ADAMS, who has been chairman of the British Institute for Strategic Studies since 1963, was one of the founders of the Institute when it was established in 1958. He is also chairman and vice-president of the British Atlantic Committee, a governor of the Atlantic Institute in Paris, and a member of the council of the Royal Institute of International Affairs in London. From 1947 to 1955, he was on the editorial staff of the London *Economist.* He is also the author of three books, the latest of which, *John Foster Dulles—A Reappraisal,* was published in the United States in 1962.

FREDERICK E. NOLTING, JR., at present vice-president of the International Division of the Morgan Guaranty Trust Company in Paris, holds the Ph.D. degree from the University of Virginia. He served in the U. S. Navy for four years during World War II, and subsequently entered the Department of State in 1946, where he served for fifteen years in various capacities—as desk officer for a number of European countries, co-ordinator of aid programs for the Far East, and assistant to the deputy undersecretary for political affairs. He has also been a member of the United States delegation to the General Assembly of the United Nations, an alternate representative to NATO, and deputy chief of the American mission to NATO. In 1961, he was appointed United States ambassador to the Republic of Viet Nam, a post that he held until 1963. His retirement from the foreign service came in the following year.

GENERAL CORTLANDT, V. R. SCHUYLER entered the U. S. Army following his graduation from the Military Academy at West Point in 1922. He served at the U. S. Antiaircraft Command at Richmond, Virginia, becoming chief of staff in 1943. In the following year, he was sent to Bucharest, Rumania, as military representative on the Allied Control Commission. In 1947, he returned to Washington to become chief of plans of the Department of the Army. In 1951, he accompanied Generals Dwight D. Eisenhower and Alfred M. Gruenther to Europe to establish the Supreme Headquarters of the Allied Powers in Europe. In 1953, he became chief of staff to General Gruenther, who had succeeded General Eisenhower as Supreme Commander. From 1956, following his promotion to full general in May, until his retirement in 1959, he acted as chief of staff under General Lauris Norstad. In 1960, Governor Nelson Rockefeller appointed him commissioner of general services of the State of New York and, in 1963, chairman of the New York State Civil Defense Commission.

SIR EVELYN SHUCKBURGH, who was educated at Winchester and King's College, Cambridge, entered the foreign service of Great Britain in 1933 and has served in the British embassies in Cairo, Ottawa, Buenos Aires, and Prague. Between 1951 and 1954, he was principal private secretary to the foreign minister, Sir Anthony Eden. From 1954 to 1956, he specialized in Middle Eastern affairs in the Foreign Office, and, from 1956 to 1958, was senior civilian instructor at the Imperial Defense College in London. In 1958, he became political secretary to the then secretary general of NATO, Paul-Henri Spaak, a position he held until 1960. In 1962, after two years with the Foreign Office, in which he concentrated on European and Atlantic affairs, he assumed his present post as the United Kingdom's permanent representative to the North Atlantic Council.

GENERAL PAUL STEHLIN, who is a graduate of the French Military Academy at Saint-Cyr and holds a diploma in higher German studies from the University of Strasbourg, served as air attaché to the French Embassy in Berlin from 1935 to 1939. During World War II, he saw action in Finland, Norway, France, Tunisia, Italy, and Germany and was commander of the French Air Force in the Mediterranean. Since the war he has held posts as air attaché in London, chief deputy to the general staff of the minister of national defense, and chief of the French delegation to the standing group of NATO in Washington. In 1960, he became chief of the general staff of the French Air Force. He is the author of a recent book, *Témoignage pour l'histoire.*

THE HONORABLE DIRK STIKKER is the retired secretary general of NATO and chairman of the North Atlantic Council. He has held posts as the Dutch permanent representative to the North Atlantic Council and chairman of the Organization for European Economic Cooperation. From 1952 to 1958, he was the Netherlands ambassador to the Court of St. James and, concurrently, from 1954 to 1958, minister and later ambassador to the Republic of Iceland. In 1955 and 1956, he was chairman of the United Nations, and from 1948 to 1952, he served as the Dutch minister of foreign affairs.